ANTIQUE BRASS & COPPER

Identification & Value Guide

Revised Edition

Ashley L. Sullivan
200 Craven St.
Beaufort, NC 28516

Mary Frank Gaston

COLLECTOR BOOKS

A Division of Schroeder Publishing Co., Inc.

To Jerry and Jeremy

The current values in this book should be used only as a guide. They are not intended to set prices, which vary from one section of the country to another. Auction prices as well as dealer prices vary greatly and are affected by condition as well as demand. Neither the Author nor the Publisher assumes responsibility for any losses that might be incurred as a result of consulting this guide.

Additional copies of this book may be ordered from:

Collector Books
P.O. Box 3009
Paducah, Kentucky 42002-3009

or

Mary Frank Gaston
P.O. Box 342
Bryan, Texas 77806

@16.95. Add $2.00 for postage and handling

Copyright: Mary Frank Gaston, 1992
Updated Values, 1994

Printed by IMAGE GRAPHICS, INC., Paducah, Kentucky

Contents

ACKNOWLEDGMENTS

I wish to thank a large number of people who contributed to this book in a variety of ways. First, I thank my publisher, Bill Schroeder, for publishing my earlier books, *Antique Brass* and *Antique Copper,* which were released in 1985. He suggested this revised work which combines the two subjects. Because the two metals have so many common characteristics and since many collectors are interested in objects made from both copper and brass, combining the two earlier books will make this new edition a more useful reference for collectors.

Second, I thank my editor, Steve Quertermous, for the many tasks he performs in seeing a book through to its completion. It has been my pleasure to work with him on several different subjects for over ten years.

Third, I thank my husband, Jerry, for photographing the majority of pieces featured in this book. Brass and copper are not easy to photograph, and he experimented with different shots and backgrounds in order to get the best prints possible. Jerry is always helpful in other aspects of getting the book ready for publication. I am lucky that he enjoys "antiquing" as much as I do.

Fourth, I thank Susan and Michael Evans, Faraway Cottage Antiques, Ontario, California. They photographed a number of pieces which have been included in this new edition which helped to add to and expand the various categories. Their work with the photographs and information about the pieces they submitted was very helpful.

A large group of collectors and dealers permitted me to photograph their collections of brass and copper for both of the earlier books, and I wish to thank them once again. Several other names have been added to this long list of contributors who supplied pieces or photographs for this edition. To each of the following, I extend a very sincere "Thank You!"

Albert's Mall
    Nashville, Indiana
Sallie Tucker Anderson, The Boll Weevil Antiques
    Calvert, Texas
Anteaque Tyme
    Dallas, Texas
The Antique Center
    San Antonio, Texas
The Antique Connection
    San Antonio, Texas
Antique Showcase
    Fredericksburg, Texas
Antiques on Main
    San Antonio, Texas
Antiques & Things, The Emporium
    Bastrop, Texas
Austin Antique Mall
    Austin, Texas
Peggy Becker
    Ontario, California
D. J. Blackburn
    Waco, Texas
Joe and Von Bolin, The Tulip & The Bird
    Fredericksburg, Texas

Bill and Toncy Brown, Granny Had It Antiques
    Dallas, Texas
Joyce Brown, Prairie Wind Antiques
    Fredrick, Oklahoma
Stella Brown, Migration Antiques
    Bryan, Texas
Helen Buchanan, The Copper Lamp
    Dallas, Texas
Peggy Burrows, The Emporium
    Bastrop, Texas
Bob Campbell, The Porch, Big D Bazaar
    Dallas, Texas
Lamar & Mabel Chambers, Let's Decorate
    Dallas, Texas
Bob & Marth Davison, Horseshoe Antiques & Gifts
    Fairplay, Colorado
Den of Steven Antique Mall
    Louisville, Kentucky
The Depot Antiques
    New Braunfels, Texas
The Drews
    Fort Worth, Texas
Maizelle Dunlap, Bessie Mai's Antiques
    Fort Worth, Texas

Eclectic Ideas
  Dallas, Texas
Kevin Edwards, Fantasia
  Dallas, Texas
Elgin Antique Mall
  Elgin, Texas
Asa & Sue Ellis Antiques
  Arlington, Texas
Donald J. Embree Antiques, Inc.
  Dallas, Texas
Linda Eulich & Isabelle Young, M.I.L.E. Galleries
  Dallas, Texas
Puddin Evans, Mondays Antiques
  Dallas, Texas
R. C. Fitzpatrick
  Sebring, Florida
Rose Flocke, The Doubletree
  Wimberley, Texas
Virginia Fresne, Precious Memories
  San Antonio, Texas
Dustin & Evelyn Gorden, The Barn Haus
  San Antonio, Texas
David Harris Antiques, Big D Bazaar
  Dallas, Texas
Jean's Antiques & Collectables
  Houston, Texas
Erwin & Jamie Hendrix, Jamie's Antiques, Big D Bazaar
  Dallas, Texas
Bill R. Lafferty, Bildor's Glasstiques
  San Antonio, Texas
Maralee & Lauren Langholz, Mara Lang's Antiques
  Mission, Texas
Elizabeth Leconey, Highland Park Antiques & Nauticles Ltd.
  Dallas, Texas
B. Lightsey
  San Antonio, Texas
Roberta McCrary, Bois d'Arc
  Calvert, Texas
The Main Place Antique Mall
  San Antonio, Texas
Esther Maldonado, Esther's Antiques
  Bandera, Texas
Martindale Antique Mall
  Martindale, Texas
Ward & Don Mayborn, Uncommon Market
  Dallas, Texas
LaDonna Mechaley, Serendipity Shop
  Rapid City, South Dakota

Barbara & Thomas Morrison, The Victory Antiques
  Dallas, Texas
Motif International
  Dallas, Texas
Deanie Nolan, Deanie's Front Parlor
  San Antonio, Texas
Rosie O'Reilly Antiques
  Austin, Texas
Our Favorite Things
  Dallas, Texas
Pendleton's Antiques & Collectibles
  San Antonio, Texas
Judith Peters, Big D Bazaar
  Dallas, Texas
Red Rooster Antique Mall
  Las Vegas, Nevada
Return Engagement
  Dallas, Texas
Nadine Reynolds
  Austin, Texas
Harvey Richman, Le Monde Antiques
  Dallas, Texas
Kathleen M. Russell, Big D Bazaar
  Dallas, Texas
The Sandbergs, New Braunfels Antiques
  New Braunfels, Texas
Faye Schoenfeld, Antiques & Interiors
  San Antonio, Texas
Leola & Edgar Schulze; Edgar B. & Connie Schulze
  Lee-Ed Antiques, Fredericksburg, Texas
Jim & Jerrie Shepard, Shep's Country Mouse
  Belton, Missouri
Betty & Bud Sparks, The Attic
  Bryan, Texas
Jean & Mike Sudderth, Country Cottage Antiques
  Fredericksburg, Texas
Bobbie Terrell, Lost Pines Antiques
  Bastrop, Texas
Treaty Oak Antique Mall
  Austin, Texas
Al & Wanda Trigg, Al's Trifles & Treasures
  Hurst, Texas
Doris Turner's Antiques
  Austin, Texas
Mary & Ray Vaughn, Mary's Antiques & Collectibles
  Louisville, Kentucky
Joe Webb & Jerry LeFevor, Paradise Antiques
  Dallas, Texas

Preface

Antique Brass

The world of brass is a fascinating topic of study. The metal, although known in prehistoric times, has continued throughout the centuries to the present day to benefit civilization in countless ways, both functional and decorative. The metal's resemblance to gold has perhaps sustained and maintained interest in brass throughout history. That is not to say that the metal has not had its critics or ups and downs in popularity. At times "brass" has had a bad connotation and been the victim of low repute, especially when the metal has been used falsely to represent gold. We have all seen old movies where someone bites a coin to be sure that the coin is in fact gold and not brass! "Brassy" is a word still used which has a degrading meaning, defined by Webster as "cheap and showy." The origin of that term appears to have come about during the late Victorian times when an abundance of brass was used by the lower classes for decoration and ornamentation!

It is apparent that brass has managed to endure and survive its critics, however. Today, tremendous amounts of new brass are imported to the United States, showing that there is a profitable market for new brass goods of all types. But most importantly, there is a very large market for old brass today because of its scarcity and the past it represents. New brass may strive to emulate and copy old brass, but there is a difference between the two, making the older pieces highly sought.

Although brass made during the first half of the twentieth century is certainly not "antique," brass of that period is now beginning to find its place on today's antique market. Many of the items from the early years of this century are obsolete in use and thus collectible for that reason. Other brass reflects the styles of the Art Nouveau and Art Deco periods of this century and merits collecting because of the distinctive styles associated with these periods. Even decorative brass items such as plaques and jardinieres featuring embossed tavern scenes and fruit themes which were popular during the 1950's are now considered collectibles.

Brass made prior to or during the seventeenth century and early eighteenth century in Europe and America is quite rare on the open market. The surviving examples from those eras have been acquired in most instances by museums or private collections. While such museum pieces are definitely important and useful in tracing the history of brass, brass from those sources has not been featured here because those items do not come within the scope of this book—to show what is currently available for sale in old brass today.

The majority of old brass available today was made during the machine age, but enough different brass items have been made to appeal to a varied group of collectors. This interest ranges from the most specialized areas of collecting such as match safes, bells, and thimbles to more general collecting fields including kitchen collectibles, nautical antiques, and railroadiana to name a few. Moreover, brass is increasingly attracting many "non-collectors" who desire old brass to add decoration and style or authenticity to their home or work place. Old brass has indeed become a coveted acquisition to a broad cross-section of the American public. Current prices reflect that demand and supply.

This book is designed to show what is currently available, basically in the realm of European and American brass, at various antique retail outlets such as shops and shows. Most of the items featured are products of the late eighteenth century through the mid twentieth century.

The introduction includes a brief historical survey of the subject, and some rudimentary facts about brass-making are discussed and defined. Tips on collecting brass and ways of differentiating between old brass and the new "repros" are also included.

Over 300 color photographs of brass objects have been divided into six broad categories. An Object Index and Value Guide are also provided to aid in locating and placing values on specific items.

By taking a look at brass manufactured over a time period of 200 plus years, we admit that the door has only been "cracked" so to speak in providing a peek into the wide world of antique and collectible brass! Hopefully, this book will serve as a useful and practical guide to that subject for both beginning and advanced collectors.

Antique Copper

Old copper, attracting varied interests, occupies a vital niche in the collector's market. Copper's enduring and attractive qualities have caused it to play an important role in the world's history. Copper articles reflecting progress through time are treasured relics by an increasing number of people. Handmade copper utensils and instruments made many hundreds of years ago are rare today; such examples are preserved mostly by museums. But an adequate supply of copper made during the last century and the early years of his century furnishes an intriguing assortment of items for today's collector.

This book focuses on those types of copper articles currently available in the antique marketplace, that is, items which can be found at antique shops, shows, antique malls, flea markets, or auctions. With few exceptions, items shown here were for sale by retail dealers and were not in personal collections.

In the introduction, the inherent characteristics of the metal, relevant historical information, and collecting notes with an emphasis on prices and current reproductions are outlined. Terms which are often used to identify certain copper objects, but whose meaning may not be clear, are also included. The Value Guide at the end of the book quotes a value range for each item shown.

More than 300 color photographs have been selected to illustrate the types of collectible copper seen most frequently for sale today. The photographs are arranged in three sections. The household copper section comprises the largest portion of the copper photographs. Examples are presented according to where such copper items might have been found in a home of the past such as the parlor and study, or kitchen and dining room. This method of illustrating was chosen over an alphabetical approach because it seemed a bit more interesting.

The commercial copper section includes trade related items pertinent to some businesses such as restaurants, newspapers, and even boot makers. Tools and instruments, used either in the field or in business, are also shown in this section.

The modern reproductions section has been emphasized in order to help collectors easily recognize several types of new copper found side-by-side with old copper at some antique outlets throughout the country. Some hints on differentiating the old and the new are also discussed in the first part of the book. An Object Index is provided in case items do not appear where you might expect them to be.

I hope you enjoy taking a step back in time to look at the nature and use of our ancestors' copper. Most of the articles are rarely used today for their intended purpose, but they furnish an interesting appreciation of the past.

Mary Frank Gaston
P.O. Box 342
Bryan, Texas 77806

Readers wishing to correspond, please include a self-addressed stamped envelope if a reply is requested.

Brass and Its Production

Brass is a metal alloy made from two natural elements, copper and zinc. Copper constitutes the bulk of the formula for making brass, ranging from about 66 percent to 83 percent. The amount of zinc added to the copper affects the resulting color of the metal and also adds strength and durability to the alloy. The optimum color for brass is considered to be a rich gold. A gold color is obtained when the zinc content ranges between 17 and 30 percent. Zinc used in proportions of over 30 percent gives the metal different colors varying from shades of white to gray. The less zinc used, the redder the color of the brass.

Brass has certain properties which make it a very useful metal. It is quite flexible and lends itself to being shaped in many different ways. Brass is harder and more durable than copper alone. Brass is not rigid and does not break easily. It is a good conductor of heat and does not rust. The alloy can also be used as a base metal for other finishes such as silver. The finish gives the look of the "real thing," but at a fraction of the cost of an item made entirely of a more precious metal, such as silver or gold.

The chief disadvantage of brass is that it should be lined with some other metal if the article is to come in contact with food. Most foods have a "tainted" taste if served from unlined brass vessels. Acidic foods can cause a reaction with the metal on direct contact and corrode the brass itself. In the early days, people were not knowledgeable of these effects. In time, they tried to correct the situation by lining brass (and copper) utensils with tin. There was still a problem though, because lead was required for the process and it was poisonous. By 1756, in England, however, the technique of tinning brass and copper without using lead was perfected (Wills, 1968, p.21). It should be pointed out that some countries still did not line all brass cooking vessels even after it was possible to use the pure tinning process. Milk containers in Holland and apple butter and candy-making kettles in America are noted examples. Eventually nickel and then stainless steel replaced tin as a lining for brass and copper cooking utensils.

A second slight disadvantage of brass is that, over time, it tarnishes from exposure to air. Thus, if one desires brass to be shiny, like gold, the items must be polished. This is easily accomplished with the aid of commercial polishes although it does require some time. Alternatively, brass can be lacquered, which will deter tarnishing and only necessitate dusting from time to time.

From the multitude of items which have been made and continue to be made from brass, it is apparent that the metal has well withstood these two disadvantages. The metal's wide diversity has enabled it to remain a very popular metal for manufacturing a wide number of both utilitarian and decorative items for hundreds of years.

Origins of Brass

Bronze was the predecessor of brass. Bronze is considered to be the oldest known metal alloy. Its discovery occurred in Mesopotamia centuries before Christ. The Bronze Age takes its name from this alloy and marks the second period in the cultural evolution through prehistoric times, succeeding the Stone Age and preceding the Iron Age.

Brass is not as old as bronze, although the actual discovery of brass (who, when, and where) is not very clear. The reason for this is because bronze and brass often were confused in ancient times as being one and the same, and sometimes they are still confused. The two alloys have the same basic ingredient: copper. But tin, rather than zinc, is combined with copper to make bronze. In most instances, the color of the two alloys is different. Bronze is usually reddish-brown while brass is gold. But when less zinc was added to brass, the color was reddish and thus similar to bronze in color. When either of the two metals was gilded, it was often impossible to distinguish between the two. Even today bronze and antique cast brass or gilded pieces are sometimes identified as the wrong alloy. A chemical analysis would be needed in most instances to determine whether the item is brass or bronze.

Brass was actually superior to bronze in several respects. Bronze was not as easy to work with as brass. Nearly all bronze items had to be cast into shape. Brass could also be cast, but its ductile nature allowed it to be fashioned in other ways from the earliest of times. The bronze alloy was easier to achieve than the brass alloy, but the workable nature of brass caused brass to surpass bronze in use through time.

Evidence confirms the fact that brass (as differentiated from bronze) had been found in remains of ruins in various parts of Europe and Asia predating modern civilization. The Roman period (27 B.C. to A.D. 395) is considered by some to be the earliest time when brass was made. Through most of the Dark or Middle Ages in Europe (A.D. 476 to 1450), the art of making brass and bronze was lost. The processes were revived to a great extent, however, by the thirteenth century.

One exception to this is the town of Dinant, in Belgium. That city had a thriving brass industry for more than 500 years. In 1466, the entire city along with its brass industry was destroyed. Aachen and then Nuremberg in Germany were also famous brass producers from the fifteenth through the seventeenth centuries. Central Europe, especially the Germanic areas and the low countries such as Belgium and Holland were well suited for the development of mineral industries. Vast mineral deposits and rivers in those regions made the locations natural for the establishment of mineral industries. The ore which contained zinc, and is of course necessary for the manufacture of brass, was especially plentiful. The proximity of these countries to each other caused the methods and techniques of making brass to be carried from country to country. By the 1600's, brass was firmly established as an important trade commodity throughout Europe and other parts of the world.

The similarity of brass to gold, both in color and flexible nature, accounts for the development and refinement of the brass-making process from Medieval times to the present. Gold has always been a much-coveted mineral. Historically, attempts have been made to make gold from other materials rather than leave the occurrence and discovery of the precious metal to the whim of nature and chance. During the Middle Ages, alchemists tried to find a formula for gold by mixing together various natural elements. Alchemy was a very secretive and mysterious process. Brass-making during this period of history was identified with the alchemists' work. The process of making brass remained cloaked in secrecy for many years. As with all secret processes, the technique was eventually passed on from one person to another, from one country to another, or discovered independently. By the seventeenth century, the method was being recorded and published. Finally, after centuries, the secrecy, mystique and magic surrounding making metals from alloys was lifted. The processes gained acceptance and recognition as a branch of true science called metallurgy.

The Manufacture of Brass

From the Middle Ages until near the end of the eighteenth century, brass-making was not an easy undertaking. The methods of extracting the minerals from their ores were crude, and the by-products given off by melting the ores were poisonous and thus hazardous for the workers. Although bronze was always made by directly fusing copper and tin, it was not possible to make brass by direct fusion in Europe until 1781. (As with other Oriental advances, China had been able to manufacture brass by direct fusion centuries earlier.)

From the Middle Ages until 1781, European brass was made by crushing the mineral ore *lapis calaminearis* to mix with the copper ore. Haedeke (1969, p. 28) notes that Europeans did not even know that zinc was the actual element in the ore. They only knew that the crushed ore, when mixed with the copper ore, would change the color of the copper. The process of crushing the zinc ore was involved and complicated. For that reason, brass centers were often located near the deposits of the *lapis calaminearis* rather than the copper sites. The copper ore was easier to obtain and transport than the zinc.

Once the two ores were properly crushed, they were heated at high temperatures until they became molten and blended. After the mixture had cooled somewhat, it could be poured into pits or onto slabs of stone. When the mixture was poured onto slabs of stone, it formed a sheet which could then be cut into strips, or the sheets could be hammered into desired thickness. The brass which was poured into pits was used for casting objects.

In that time period, without benefit of advanced technology, brass-making was often a "hit or miss" activity. It was not possible to control the measurements of the ingredients or the temperatures for melting the ores. As a result, the quality, texture, and color of the brass often would vary greatly. Great skill, time, and effort were necessary to produce brass. Nonetheless, from the rather crude and inexact techniques of the Middle Ages, many brass articles were made in this manner up through most of the eighteenth century. But with practice came expertise and improvements. Such experimentation leading to improved methods of manufacture was warranted because of the continued demand for brass items of all types. The metal was functional, and its resemblance to gold helped to brighten up the mostly dark and drab homes of the middle classes.

Early methods of shaping brass were beating or hammering the cooled molten metal. This was done by hand in the early days and later by water powered machinery. Objects were literally beaten into the desired shape such as a kettle or a pan. "Battery Works" became the name coined for locations where brass was made. From an early time, brass was also drawn into wire and made into pins. The wire was used to make the teeth in wool-cards. Such cards were essential for obtaining yarn from raw wool. Brass pins, of course, had many uses and were a great improvement over inferior wire that had been used in the past.

There were several ways of casting brass objects. One was called the lost wax (*cire perdue*) method. That technique was replaced by sand casting during the 1700's. Brass could be cast solidly, that is with no hollow center, and much early brass was cast in that manner. Later, brass was cast in two parts and soldered together. Core-casting was an improvement over two-part casting because the article could be cast in one piece with a hollow core.

As well as being a relatively easy metal to shape, brass also could be decorated with various designs applied in a number of ways. Chased and engraved designs, pierced patterns, and repoussé work were popular methods, accomplished at first by hand and later by machines.

The English Brass Industry

Although brass was and is made in many parts of

the world, the English brass industry had the greatest impact on the development of brass-making after the seventeenth century. England was late, in relation to the other European countries, in becoming involved in making brass. During the eighteenth century, however, the country became famous the world over for the finest brass made. Many improvements in manufacturing brass were developed and patented in England during the eighteenth century, and thus it is important to take special note of England's part in any discussion concerning the history of brass. England also had a direct influence on the development of brass-making in America. Moreover, many items which are available for collectors today are of English origin, which further makes the history of English brass pertinent to American collectors.

The detailed history of England's brass industry is quite fascinating and has been well documented by several English authors. Some titles in the bibliography are recommended for those interested in reading about that somewhat colorful part of English history. For our purposes, we will limit the discussion to several facts which are considered basic knowledge for brass collectors.

Until the latter part of the sixteenth century, England relied on imported brass from other European countries, especially Holland, to supply her needs. That situation began to change when Queen Elizabeth I of England began her reign in 1558. The Queen was responsible for opening the way for England's entry into the brass industry. She realized that England must become independent in as many ways as possible in order to remain a sovereign power. Most importantly, it was necessary for the country to be able to make its own weapons and tools of defense. For armaments, metals were needed. The first step toward such independence was to bring all of the mineral mines in England under royal ownership. That was accomplished in 1568. The Society of Mineral and Battery Works was also established at that time to manufacture articles from metals, especially arms. The royal monopoly of the mines and manufacturing lasted almost one hundred years, until England's Civil War with Scotland in 1642. That war brought about the collapse of England's brass industry as well as the destruction of most of the available brass objects, which were melted down to make more arms (Gentle and Feild, 1975).

The Civil War ended in 1649, but the British brass industry did not get back on its feet for almost 40 years. In 1688, William of Orange (William III) became England's first constitutional monarch. In the next year, the Mines Royal Act was passed which took control of the mines out of the hands of royalty. Thus individual ownership of mines and metal manufacturing became possible. Consequently, brass-making in England began once more in earnest.

During the eighteenth century, many towns in England manufactured brass, but Birmingham became the best known center of the English brass industry. Throughout that century, England made and exported a tremendous amount of brass of all types. As early as 1699, England prohibited her American colonies from performing any type of manufacturing, including that of brass, thus assuring a large and constant market for her products in that part of the world. But English brass gained renown abroad as well.

During the 1700's, events occurred in the English brass industry which revolutionized the manufacturing process and eventually brought about its total industrialization. The two most important events were the discovery of distilling pure zinc in 1738 by William Champion and the discovery of making brass by the direct fusion of copper and zinc in 1781 by James Emerson. Distilling pure zinc eliminated the tedious process of obtaining the metal from crushing the *lapis calaminearis* stone. Distillation made it possible to have pure zinc in the form of ingots. The direct fusion technique (43 years later) was the real breakthrough for the industry. That technique enabled the manufacturing process to be controlled, which resulted in a standard quality and color of brass. The best English brass was said to have a composition of one quarter zinc to three quarters copper. That formula resulted in the best gold color.

Several other important patents were issued in England during the 1700's which also played a decisive role in the industrialization of the brass industry. A patent for rolling brass by machines was a vast improvement over beating the metal into sheets and shapes. A stamp and die method of placing patterns and designs on brass was patented by John Pickering in 1769. That invention replaced the necessity of decorating brass totally by hand. In 1777, John Marston was able to stamp out small items entirely by using the basic principle developed by Pickering. Eventually it was possible to stamp out larger items, and soon stamping largely replaced casting as a method of shaping brass objects. The discovery of steam power by James Watt in 1769 was adapted to brass-making machinery during the 1780's. By the beginning of the 1800's, Britain's brass industry was definitely industrialized.

Mechanization of the brass industry meant that a large number of different items could be produced quickly, cheaply, and efficiently. Mass production was good on the one hand because it allowed production to keep pace with demand and because more people could afford the products. On the other hand, such an abundance of brass at lower prices was responsible for the metal losing its appeal among the middle classes. Brass became cheapened in the eyes of many and began to be considered less desirable. Although the machine-made brass produced during the early 1800's retained the fine qualities associated with earlier English brass, and in spite of the fact that earlier brass was considered superior to those products made by machines, many fine brass pieces from those earlier times were thrown out, melted down, or stored away to be out of sight and forgotten during the 1800's (see

Gentle and Feild, 1975, p. 57). Luckily some of those pieces were saved and salvaged by astute collectors in later years.

English brass made prior to 1800, before total mechanization of the industry had arrived, remains scarce. Many examples which have been discovered are in museums today. Occasionally a few of those early items surface on today's market. Things that go out of style have a way of coming back in vogue after a period of time, often on a higher level of appreciation and hence value) than when they were first made—Tiffany lamps are a good American example of that type of trend. Such examples of English eighteenth century brass are of course highly desirable when found, and if one can pay the price.

Many historians and antiquarians consider that only brass made in England before about 1850 should be classified as truly antique brass and merit consideration for a collection. The era of machine-made antiques and collectibles has definitely arrived, however. Furniture, glass, and all types of ceramics are just a few categories where this is true, especially among American collectors. Machine-made brass is another one of those categories.

Because of a lack of supply of earlier items, those who appreciate the metal for its aesthetic qualities turn to English brass made during the late 1800's through the early and even up to the mid 1900's. Many of those articles are more than 100 years old or close to that age while others are definitely "collectible." Brass from that period is relatively plentiful. Some prices are even quite high, but overall a sufficient quantity of brass of that vintage is available which not only spans a broad range of collector interest, but also spans a broad range of pocketbooks!

The American Brass Industry

Earlier, I noted that England prohibited America from carrying on any type of manufacturing after 1699 and until about 1776). Brass had been made in the colonies on a limited scale prior to that time, and the new law did not really put an end to the brass-making that was being done. The law was a difficult one to enforce. Most of the people in America who were making brass did so as a cottage-type industry. At that time the colonists did not have access to the raw materials for making brass. The brass made was by people called "braziers" who used scrap brass, bits and pieces of old or worn out imported brass. The scrap metal was melted down and new items formed. The braziers often traveled around from place to place plying their trade.

Most American brass of that period was of a utilitarian, rather than decorative nature. Its uses were mainly for lighting, heating, cooking, and washing—the basic necessities of life. Any item made of brass was important for any household. Brass was highly esteemed in the early American home and remained popular for a much longer time than it did in England. In fact, brass possessions were an indication of prestige and owned by the wealthy in the colonies whereas in England, the metal was owned mainly by the middle classes. All brass was treated with great care and passed on from one generation to another. Many examples show signs of careful mending.

It is generally agreed that brass-making on more than just a modest scale did not gain any great momentum until after the Revolutionary War. Even after the war, when the colonists were no longer forbidden by law to engage in that type of industry, it was still not easy to make brass from "scratch." The minerals had to be imported, especially zinc, and native copper was not mined to any great extent during that period. As a result, much American brass continued to be made from scrap. As more and more people emigrated to America from England and Europe, many brought advanced knowledge and skill in making the metal itself and thus helped to widen the industry in this country. Eventually some brass-making was carried on in most colonies. Pennsylvania and Connecticut were among the most prolific. All types of brass were manufactured. Brass buttons were very popular, and of course, all kinds of kettles and cooking utensils were made. Early American brass was made by sand casting or by hammering sheet brass. A new method of shaping brass was introduced in the 1850's by H.W. Hayden. He developed a technique for spinning brass which made the articles much lighter in weight, which was especially important for large cooking kettles and pans. This particular method of making brass was practiced to a large extent in Connecticut, and many of the pieces were signed by the makers (Ketchum, 1980, pp. 142-143). Signed brass from this period is quite rare because brass made in Europe or America was seldom marked prior to the late nineteenth and early twentieth centuries.

Although America was free to make brass after 1776, and the industry did grow, much foreign-made brass, including English brass, was still imported. Historically, that situation has not changed because foreign brass has always been less expensive to produce than American brass, and thus the price has been cheaper. The industry in this country has not been able to compete too profitably with the imported products. Therefore American-made brass is relatively scarce in comparison with brass made in other countries.

Collecting Brass

This book focuses primarily on European and American brass rather than brass of other origins. Collectible or "old" brass is considered to be any brass product made through the mid twentieth century, circa the 1950's. Brass made prior to the twentieth century is of course more desirable, but such examples are quite scarce today, and when available are quite expensive. Many items made in brass during the early part of this century merit collector status because the piece is unique or obsolete. Brass made as late as the second quarter of this century is now more than 40 years old and thus considered collectible. Examples are more plentiful from this period and are usually fairly easy to distinguish from current imports and the "repros" which are on the market today.

Objects made of brass have been collected as a source of pleasure, curiosity about the past, a link with history, and as an investment by serious collectors for many years. Interest in brass today, however, spans many collecting areas and is not confined to brass collectors per se. Brass plays an important part in general metal collections which may also include copper, tin, and pewter. Many collectors especially like to concentrate on copper and brass for a collection. One reason for this is because many articles were made by combining the two metals. A dipper or bedwarmer may have a copper bowl but a brass handle, or sometimes copper and brass were used to achieve a decorative effect. The two metals complement each other and make attractive displays.

Collectors of tools and scientific instruments compete in the search for brass. Navigational equipment contains many items made of brass, and many collectors are interested in the subject of nautical antiques. Kitchen collectibles of all kinds are rapidly gaining interest among a large segment of the collecting public. Brass, of course, finds a place in that particular area.

But most importantly, old brass has broken out of the bounds of antique collecting into even more general demand by persons who might not be termed "antiquers" or "collectors" at all. The concern and interest in home decoration has been responsible in a large way for bringing antique brass to the high status of attraction it is currently enjoying. Interior design and decoration has become a big business in the United States. Many books and magazines are totally devoted to illustrating ways to make the American home attractive as well as functional. Decorating firms are located in cities and towns all over the country. Brass is recognized as a metal which can bring warmth, charm, and style into a home of any size. Brass accent for totally decorative purposes fit well into the most modern homes and apartments. Most of the brass pieces in such instances take on a use different from what they were originally intended to do. Coal scuttle hold dried floral and leaf arrangements; cooking kettles and pans may hang on a kitchen wall but are not for use—only looks; and yacht tie-downs and sextant in wooden cases may serve as paperweights and book ends, respectively. While new brass items can and may fit the need or achieve the look just as well and perhaps at a fraction of the cost, many people prefer the old, and are willing to pay top prices for just the right object.

Older homes are regaining popularity on the home-buyers market. New owners often wish to restore the homes to their original period as much as possible. Authentic brass hardware and lighting fixtures are in demand for such purposes where they serve functional needs in addition to being decorative and "period." Over the last few years, there has been mounting interest and trend in building new homes in Victorian styles. Thus another market opens for brass fixtures and accessories. There are even those individuals who have opted for getting back to basics in earnest, especially to conserve energy and fight inflation. They really use many of the earlier methods of lighting, heating, and cooking, thus widening the demand for old brass in the way of kerosene lamps and lanterns, fireplace tools, footmen and trivets, and kettles and pails of all types. A very wide umbrella does indeed cover the many interests in brass today!

Sources and Availability

Because of the ever growing interest in brass of all types coupled a few years ago with the increase in the price of the base metal, copper, old brass is becoming harder to find and prices are high and getting higher. Newcomers to brass collecting might wonder just how much old brass is presently available today, and where the sources are for such pieces.

Early American brass is much more scarce than brass of other origins. Examples which definitely can be authenticated as American are mostly in museums today or in the hands of advanced collectors and not available on the open market. The United States still remains a hunting ground and source of old brass however. Collectors can scour small shops and out-of-the-way places and find genuinely old items which have been in this country (even if perhaps not made here) for a hundred years or more. They will be more uccessful, or course, in finding brass made during the late nineteenth and early twentieth centuries.

The largest supply and source of old brass on the American market is still England. For several years, huge cartons of English antiques of various types have been imported into this country. Whereas many dealers historically have gone abroad to select and bring back European antiques for American customers, the large shipments came about in response to the greatly accelerated interest in antiques by the general public over the last 15 or so years. Many brass items arrive in these lots. Some of the pieces are definitely old and have been salvaged from Britain's eighteenth and early nineteenth century brass industry. Others are objects made as late as the 1940's and 1950's. Most of the pieces are in fact English, but some are of other European origin. Similar containers are also being imported from France, Holland, Portugal, and Spain. Such shipments are sold to antique dealers throughout the United States. More and more, large shops are relying on this source of supply to meet the needs of their customers. A variety of interesting brass items will usually be found at such locations.

Metal stripping shops are another source of old brass. Many metal items such as brass and copper were plated with another metal at one time. Today the underlying metal is much more valuable and attractive than the plated items which have begun to show signs of wear and are relatively expensive to re-plate. Special shops focus on stripping such ware as well as polishing and lacquering the pieces in the process. Often these businesses operate as retail outlets as well as performing the service for individually owned items. Trays, kettles, fire extinguishers, and all types of hardware are some examples which may be found for sale.

In the same way, to some extent, brass hardware and lighting fixtures can be found in businesses specializing in architectural antiques. All types of fixtures have been rescued from older homes in this country which were about to be demolished for "progress." Windows, flooring, mantels, columns, ceiling fans, and sometimes whole rooms can be located at these stores in addition to hardware and lighting fixtures. The prices are often quite competitive with new fixtures. Many businesses today specialize in making new hardware which looks old and can be used to complete old items lacking drawer pulls, key holes, and knobs, but if one desires, authentic old pieces for those purposes can still be found.

Old and New Brass

The early brass-makers did not furnish precise clues to enable collectors years later to attribute a specific brass object to a specific maker or even to a specific origin. English brass of the seventeenth and eighteenth centuries was not required to be marked even though English silver was. Similarly, American makers also rarely marked their brass. During the latter part of the nineteenth century, and on through the twentieth century, brass was marked more often by the manufacturer because of the stamping process. "England" or "Made in England" is often seen on later English brass, even if there is not a name of a particular manufacturer. Thus it is indeed a "find" if a marked example of English or American brass is found made prior to the late 1800's or early 1900's. Collectors are advised that a name on a piece of brass does not necessarily mean that the item was made by that person. Many people had their name engraved or placed on their brass possessions to indicate ownership. Furthermore, a name without a specific location, such as a town or a country, cannot be used definitely to identify origin of the object.

Styles or shapes of brass also cannot be used conclusively for dating brass. English brass imitated earlier European styles and American brass copied English designs. Because English brass often was made along the lines of English silver, hallmarked silver items have been used as guidelines for dating early English brass. That method is not foolproof. Even though a brass object may look just like a dated silver item in shape or design, that does not mean that the brass was made at the same time. It probably was made at least somewhat later, though it may be styled along the lines popular during a certain period—Georgian or Queen Anne for example. Although brass copied the silver styles, brass itself from those periods also has been copied. Today many of the "copies" are quite old and are collected appropriately as old brass.

During the eighteenth century, the English had pattern books illustrating brass items. These books were similar to what we would call catalogs, and were used by salesmen to show the type and variety of brass items available and their prices. The catalogs were rarely dated, but they illustrate what was being made in brass during that century even though exact years cannot be pinpointed. Old paintings showing brass objects have been suggested as another means of dating brass. Such examples may convey that certain items and styles in brass were being made during the time the piece of art was painted but such evidence is not conclusive. The same is true when comparing an item to one found in a museum. Unless the item is marked just like the one featured in the museum, the same style cannot definitely identify the item as one by the same maker or from the same time period or same origin.

Type of item is also not a clue to the age or origin of brass. Most objects of brass have been made for years, copied again and again by European and American brassmakers. A few items, however, are noted to be especially indigenous to a particular area. Objects with hinged lids are thought to be European and not American. Andirons were more prevalent in America than in England because from a very early time England heated with coal rather than wood. Samovars are considered Russian, Turkish, or Far Eastern in origin rather than West European. Apple butter kettles appear to be an American invention.

New brass from all over the world continues to flood the American market today. There are stores which sell only new brass. All furniture, gift, jewelry, and discount houses, as well as variety stores, stock a large selection of new brass. These new items generally do not pretend to be old or antique although they may be fashioned along traditional lines. Some importers, however, have items made that definitely replicate what collectors consider "old" brass objects. Candle-holders, tea kettles, jelly kettles, trivets, coal scuttles, school bells and so forth are some examples. Among collectors, such items are termed "repros" because the articles have been made to resemble genuinely old items which are being sold on the antique market. In most instances, the "repros" are sold at many of the locations where authentic antiques also are sold, such as flea markets, antique shops and antique malls. The new pieces are solid brass. They may have a paper label saying where they were made (often Taiwan). The labels do not remain on for long, and thus to the unsuspecting buyer, the item may be thought to be old.

In some ways the great influx of new brass and especially the "repros" has been somewhat detrimental to old brass collecting. As in Victorian times in England, there is so much new brass available that those searching for the old sometimes begin to feel that the old has become somewhat cheapened in the process. But from my personal observations and discussions with collectors and dealers, it is apparent that there is really never a problem in selling old brass. A large segment of the collecting public is still determined to turn their backs on the new and the "repros" and diligently search for the older pieces.

Tips on Identifying Old Brass
If old brass cannot be dated easily because it is not marked and because decorative styles and types of items also cannot be definitive as dating guidelines, just how can one differentiate old brass from new brass? From talking with brass collectors and dealers, it is apparent that not being able to date a brass object specifically does not hinder the collector. Brass collectors are not rigid in demanding that brass must be signed, marked or noted as having been made at an exact time. Collections would be very limited and not affordable for most collectors if that were the case. By an understanding of the past through reading books, visiting museums, discussions with others with similar interests, and by being aware and alert to the new brass, the collector becomes aware of certain clues that help in distinguishing the old from the new. These methods are the most thorough way and best protection against getting "stung" in any area of collecting.

Some suggestions or "rules of thumb" can be used to help distinguish between new brass or "repros" and brass made prior to the mid-twentieth century. The weight of the brass is a good starting point. Old brass, including late nineteenth century and early twentieth century brass, is heavier than brass currently manu-factured. New brass is thinner and sharper because the brass is rolled much more thinly. New cast brass is also usually lighter in weight. Compare new cast brass hardware to older pieces, for example.

Examine the object in detail. Look for signs of wear and smooth edges on old brass. Inspect the bails or handles on kettles and pails. These were usually made of iron and rounded, although some were also made of brass. New bails on the "repros" are often just a thin strip of flat metal. See how the piece is constructed. Was it made on one piece, are the sides seamed, is the bottom dovetailed? In older pieces, the soldering metal may show slightly in the seams, but beware of items where soldering is too obvious. Soldering is usually noticeable in dovetail construction, but that method of manufacture is too time-consuming and costly today.

Signs of mending such as on the bottom of pans and kettles indicate that pieces are old. Because many cooking utensils were lined with tin, evidence of the tinning should remain (unless the piece has been stripped). Brass is also sturdy and does not damage easily. If the piece is dented, try to determine if the dent occurred in the past or if the object has been "newly" dented to look old.

Be aware that some brass pieces have been painted over the surface. I once found a beautiful double student lamp which had been covered with gold spray paint (not gilded!). I imagine the piece had tarnished badly, and the paint was the solution to the discoloration and a remedy for polishing! But from the style of the lamp, I thought the piece should be brass, and when my magnet did not attract at any point, I bought it. Sure enough, the paint came off with paint remover, and after being cleaned and polished, I had a beautiful brass lamp!

Brass that has not been polished acquires a patina over time, eventually turning the metal a dark color. Sometimes this patina is a useful guide in telling whether brass is old or new. The patina is often so dark that the piece may look more like bronze, or it may look like a cheaper metal alloy. Don't overlook such pieces which may not readily catch your eye because they are not shiny and gold like brass. New brass also has a tendency to turn red or pinkish in color as it tarnishes rather than acquiring the dark patina of old brass.

Most new brass is lacquered to keep the metal from tarnishing, but lacquered examples do not mean that the item is new. Some people do not like the dark patina. They prefer the rich gold look plus the fact that lacquered pieces do not have to be polished. Dealers tell me that although it is an added expense and thus increases the price of an item, most customers prefer to purchase old brass which has already been lacquered. Lacquering brass is not a new technique but has been used for hundreds of years. Old brass which was lacquered many years ago, however, will now have signs of the lacquer wearing off, if it has not worn off already.

Always remember to take a magnet along when searching for old brass. Some items are merely brass plated. If the magnet does not attract, the piece is solid brass. Some items, such as lamps, however may have an iron bar through the center which will attract the magnet. In such instances, one should check out the other parts of the lamp as well.

Price is often another indicator in determining whether brass is old or new. Most new brass is relatively cheap when compared with prices for old brass. It is still possible to find some real bargains in old brass today, however. Some new finely made brass is also quite high in price. Examples of the latter do not usually cause confusion with the old because they are offered for sale by department stores or specialty catalogs where it is obvious that new merchandise is sold.

The "repros" that are so much in evidence at various "antique" locations are decidedly cheaper than the authentic item, although over the past few years the prices have been increasing. I suppose that is in response to the fact that genuinely old objects are becoming more expensive. Once in a while, a "repro" will have a price tag equal to that of its older counterpart. I am sure some people purchase such pieces thinking they are getting a true antique or collectible. But if a school bell is $15.00 or a jelly kettle $35.00 or a pair of candleholders $17.50, it is usually safe to assume that the objects are new.

Be suspicious when you see a whole lot of identical objects such as coal scuttles, jelly kettles, trivets, or ships' lanterns in the same place or identical items in gift shops, flea markets, or antique malls. The "delft-type" handle on some brass is an instant clue that the piece is new.

Do not hesitate to ask questions of dealers. Most are quite willing and happy to tell you what they know about an object such as where they bought the piece, what it was used for, and what period of time they think that it was made. Shops importing from England or other parts of Europe often have very good background information concerning those articles. Dealers who carry new or "gift" items as well as antiques will usually tell you which pieces are new or old if you ask. Sometimes they will volunteer the information when they notice you are interested in a particular object. Make friends with the dealer, and you will benefit from the dealer's knowledge and expertise.

Please note that most of the brass illustrated in this book was made during the latter part of the nineteenth century or early part of the twentieth century. Therefore dates are not shown in the captions for most photographs. If the pieces were made at other times, the captions may indicate time periods such as eighteenth century, early to mid 1800's, or mid-twentieth century (1925-1950). Remember it is usually possible to date brass only according to approximate time periods.

Major Categories of Collectible Brass

Of the multitude of objects that have been made of brass over the past several centuries, it would be impossible indeed to show or discuss examples of each one. Several hundred photographs representing a wide range of brass items are featured in this book to give a broad view of what is currently available on today's market. I have used six categories (listed below) for the brass presented in this book. Obviously some items may fit into more than one category. Many of the items in a particular category could easily constitute a book alone—candleholders or andirons, for example. An Object Index is provided at the end of the book so that readers may look there for specific items if the object in question is not immediately visible in one of the categories, or to see if a particular item has been included in the book. Although I have tried to show a representative sample of brass items in each category, I certainly do not claim to have completely covered this vast subject!

Note that some of the items shown are made only partly of brass. Brass items were combined with other metals and even wood. Brass was used in this way because it was necessary to the function of the piece, or its use was to enhance the beauty and exhibit signs of fine workmanship on the object.

1. *Lighting Implements*. Brass lighting implements are one of the most popular areas of brass collecting. They are both useful and decorative. Candleholders, candelabra, wall sconces, kerosene lamps, and table lamps are included. Chandeliers are not featured due to the breadth of that subject alone, but collectors should be aware that a wide variety of beautiful brass chandeliers is available, especially at businesses specializing in architectural antiques, and at stripping shops. Prices are quite competitive with new chandeliers.

2. *Fireplace Accessories*. A look at objects in this category probably makes us grateful for central heating and the ability to enjoy bits of the past for decor without having to use everything that was once connected with fires and the hearths in the past. Firedogs, andirons, fenders, fireplace tools, coal buckets, wood boxes, screens, footmen and trivets are some of the items featured. Remember the fireplace in the kitchen was the center of activity in most homes. Its use was not only for giving warmth, but during certain periods it was used for lighting and cooking as well. Brass used for cooking at the fireplace, however, is included in the following section on Kitchen Collectibles.

3. *Kitchen Collectibles*. Large kettles and pans for cooking, and smaller kitchen tools were often made of brass or partly of brass. It appears that more utilitarian kitchen items were made of copper rather than brass, however. Serving pieces which would probably have been found in the dining room such as coffee services, tea pots and burners, and trays are shown in this section also. Some of these latter items were once silver plated.

4. *Tools and Instruments*. Brass was well suited for certain tools and scientific instruments because of its strength and non-rusting qualities. Various trade

tools and instruments are shown. A fairly large section of nautical items is also presented. A few examples of furniture made from some of these tools are also included.

5. *Hardware Fixtures*. Practically any type of hardware for all purposes was made in brass. Door bells, mailboxes, furniture mounts (ormolu), curtain tiebacks, drawer pulls, and locks are just a few. Old brass hardware is, of course, functional, but interesting examples can also make attractive accent pieces or form a unique display.

6. *Decorative and Personal Objects*. This category covers a very broad spectrum and could be expanded indefinitely. Many of the pieces illustrated were originally designed to be functional as well as decorative. Mirrors (frames), desk and writing items, smoking accessories, and even bird cages are such examples. Plaques, jardinieres and vases have always served a decorative purpose. Some personal items such as the bidet were once totally functional, but now purely decorative, I'm sure!

Prices

A price range is quoted for each brass item illustrated in this book. Several factors always play a part in the final purchasing price of any antique or collectible. The overall condition of the item is important. Whether it has been mended, has new parts, or is missing a part are important considerations. For brass, not only those factors, but also whether the piece has been lacquered or stripped and lacquered, or if it has been made into a lamp or a piece of furniture will add to the price. Older items and unusual pieces are expected to bring higher prices than more common or later pieces. Signed examples from early periods command a premium, and American-made brass is usually favored in this country, and thus may be higher in price than brass of other origins. Additionally, prices are higher or lower in various regions of the country and may vary even within the same area. Sometimes articles at auctions sell much higher or lower than the same type objects at shops and shows depending on the particular attendance at the auction. Remember there is never a "set" price for any antique or collectible, and compared with many areas of collecting — this is especially true for brass because it is diversified in so many ways. Ultimately it is up to the individual to decide if the price is right. In essence, it is the individual as well as the dealer who sets prices based simply on the law of supply and demand.

Useful Terms

When reading and studying about various subjects, certain technical words are often used which are pertinent to the specific subject. Sometimes a word may have a different meaning than its usual definition when used in connection with some specific topic. The following list of words with brief definitions may be encountered in the study of brass. These words deal with the metal itself and relate chiefly to either the manufacture or decoration of the metal.

Alchemy—the Medieval form of chemistry in which elements, especially various metals, were mixed together in the search for gold. The practitioner of this was known as an alchemist.

Alloy—the combination of two or more metals to make another metal. Alloys are made for various purposes such as to increase strength and durability of a metal, change its appearance, or make the base metal less expensive.

Battery Works—an early name applied to the location where brass was made and shaped into objects.

Beaten Brass—refers either to the process of beating the molten brass into sheets or into objects. The term may also refer to designs made on brass objects by hammering.

Brass—a metal alloy composed of copper and zinc and very ductile in nature.

Brasses—this word may describe small items made of brass, but it frequently refers to monuments for graves used in England during the Middle Ages which were made of brass.

Brazier—may refer to persons who make brass or to containers, sometimes made of brass, for coal-made fires.

Brazing—the technique of joining metals together with a metal or a metal alloy.

Bronze—a metal alloy composed of copper and tin.

Cast—to form or shape an object by using a mold.

Chasing—a method of decorating brass with designs in relief by the use of tools to chisel or hammer the metal.

Core Casting—a technique of casting brass in one piece with a hollow core rather than casting an object into halves which must be soldered together.

Corrode—in reference to brass, the word means to destroy the metal through contact with a chemical agent.

Distill—a process to extract one substance from another, such as extracting the element of pure zinc from its ore.

Die—a metal press used for stamping shapes and designs on brass.

Doré—a French term for gilding brass or bronze. The English word for this method of decoration is *ormolu*.

Dovetail—a method of construction where the metal is cut with extensions on one part which fit into similar open spaces of another part. Evidence of this type of work can be found on some brass items such as kettles and pans. The two parts would have been soldered together.

Ductile—malleable or flexible, easy to shape and able to accommodate stress during the shaping process.

Electroplating—a process of covering an object, frequently brass or copper, with a metal coating (often silver) accomplished by using electric currents.

Element—a substance found in nature which cannot be chemically decomposed, such as gold, copper, silver, zinc.

Embossed—designs applied to brass by hammering the pattern from the inside of the object or applying a design to the exterior to achieve a raised effect. The French term for this type of work is *repoussé*.

Enameling—a decorative technique that uses a vitreous substance in various colors which is applied by fusion to brass objects.

Engraving—a method of decorating brass by cutting or carving designs into the metal.

Flat Ware—normally means objects without a hollow center such as forks, knives, and spoons as well as objects with flat surfaces such as plates and trays.

Friable—easily broken, will not tolerate stress. Bronze is friable whereas brass is not.

Fusion—the method of blending two elements together to make one, such as fusing copper and zinc to make brass.

Gilt or Gilding—the process of applying a thin coating of gold which has been mixed with mercury and then fired onto the surface of a brass or bronze object.

Hammered Brass—this term is similar to *beaten brass*, indicating that the metal was either hammered into shape or that various designs were hammered into the brass.

Hollow Ware—refers to objects which have a hollow center such as pitchers, tea and coffee pots, cups, etc.

Lacquered—the application of a thin coat of varnish to the surface of a brass object to prevent the metal from tarnishing and becoming discolored.

Latten—a word used to describe sheet brass.

Lapis Calaminearis—the natural ore containing the metal zinc.

Lost Wax—a method of casting brass in Medieval times used commercially through the seventeenth century. In this process, a model of the object was made of wax and then covered with clay. After the clay mold had hardened, it was heated at a high temperature, thus melting or "losing" the wax mold. The clay mold was then filled with molten brass. When the brass had cooled, the clay mold was broken away leaving the brass object. The French term for this process was *Cire Perdue*.

Metallurgy—the science of metals, or making metals from alloys, or extracting metals from their natural ores.

Mold or Mould—to shape an object. For brass, molds were made of clay, wax, and sand.

Molten—the state of a substance melted by high heat.

Ormolu—gilded pieces of brass or bronze used to decorate furniture. Sometimes the brass alloy was applied as decoration without gilding because of its own resemblance to gold in color. The French term for this method of decoration is *doré*.

Patina—the surface of an object such as brass that darkens with time and exposure to the air. A patina may also be achieved through the results of polishing over time. Brass may also acquire a patina by being handled over a long period without any polishing.

Pierced—a method of decorating brass with openwork designs punched into the metal.

Plated—to cover a metal or metal alloy with another metal or alloy. Brass was often plated with silver, and other materials have been plated with brass (see Electroplating). Plating allows only a small amount of the more expensive metal to be used over a cheaper metal while giving the appearance that the item is made entirely of the more expensive metal.

Punched—a technique of decorating brass by a tool that perforates the surface or may just indent the surface without perforation.

Repoussé—designs made in relief on brass (see Embossed).

Sand Casting—a method of casting brass which largely replaced the "Lost Wax" method during the eighteenth century. The technique is still in use today, especially for casting bronze. A wooden mold is made and placed in a special container which has been filled with a wet sand substance. The sand is packed tightly around the mold. After the wooden model has made its impression into the sand, it is removed. The sand must become dry and harden; then the molten metal can be poured into the mold, eventually resulting in the metal object.

Sheet Brass—molten brass which, after cooling, was beaten into thin sheets by hand at first and later by water-powered hammers until the rolling machine was invented during the early 1700's.

Smelt—to melt metals or ores containing metals, or to make alloys by melting two or more metals together such as copper and zinc to form brass.

Solder—to join together with a molten metal alloy or metal, such as soldering the sides of a candlestick.

Solid Casting—the shaping of a brass object without a hollow core.

Spun Brass—a technique of shaping brass with the use of a die and rotating device resulting in lighter weight brass objects such as kettles and pans.

Stamping—the process of making either designs on brass or stamping out the object completely by using a metal die.

Tarnish—refers to a metal losing its shine and becoming discolored, as through oxidation.

Tin—a metal used alone, or with other metals to make alloys. For example, copper and tin are combined to make bronze. Tin was also used to line brass cooking ware and eating utensils in the past because it prevented a "tainted" taste from direct contact of brass with food; also, it kept acidic foods from corroding the brass.

Zinc—a natural element used with copper to make the alloy brass.

Copper and Its Production

Copper is a basic metallic element derived from mineral ores occurring naturally in the Earth's surface. The metal is essentially soft although it is stronger than gold. Copper is thus malleable and easy to shape. The metal is very attractive in its natural reddish-brown color, although its color may vary from pink, to a deep rust, or to a bright red. Its polished surface reflects light and takes on a pleasing glow and patina through use and polishing over time.

Copper does not rust, but it can corrode, especially in contact with acidic substances. Verdigris, a blue-green coating, develops on copper when it is exposed to the elements over long periods. That type of discoloration is evident on buildings with copper roofs. The verdigris can be removed, but it will eventually return. The coating, however, does not harm the metal seriously.

Cleaning copper does not require an inordinate amount of effort, nor must it be done frequently. Commercial copper polishes quickly restore a warm sheen that will remain for some time. Also, pieces can be protected by a coat of lacquer. Then they need only periodic dusting. Many collectors of old copper, however, usually prefer the natural patina which pieces acquire over time.

Copper is very durable. It really does not wear out. When objects do become worn, they can be patched or reseamed. Alternatively, the worn pieces can be melted, and some new item fashioned from the scrap metal.

Copper is a good conductor of heat. Centuries ago, copper vessels were used for cooking. Copper cooking ware remains popular even today. In modern times, the metal was discovered also to be a good conductor of electricity, being used extensively in electrical wiring.

Copper is an essential ingredient in manufacturing several metal alloys. Those alloys are stronger than copper, and thus greatly diversify the use of the metal. Bronze, made by combining copper with tin, is thought to be the first man-made alloy. Copper and tin, in different proportions than used to make bronze, produce other alloys such as bell metal, gun metal, pewter, and Britannia metal. Brass, composed of copper and zinc, appears to be the most widely used copper alloy. Because of copper's characteristics, it is easy to see why the metal has played such an important role in the development of modern civilization up to present times.

The metal has been known from very early times in all parts of the world. Copper and gold are, in fact, considered to be the first metals known to man, although history cannot pinpoint the date or the location of the first discovery of either. Archeological sites have yielded evidence that copper was used by the ancient civilizations of China, Egypt, Greece, and Rome. Copper tools, weapons and cooking vessels were common in Europe during the Middle Ages. North American Indians possessed copper-made articles when the continent was discovered by Europeans.

Although copper's history can be traced to prehistoric times and to various parts of the world, relevant historical information for today's American collector centers for the most part on English and American copper. England was the largest source of copper-made articles for American colonists. England's copper industry, however, did not develop on any large scale until the beginning of the eighteenth century. Previously, England had relied on imported copper from Germany and Holland, either in the form of ready-made items, or in the raw material which could be worked into objects.

In 1689, the Mines Royal Act took control of the mines away from the Crown, and as a result, it became possible for individuals to own mines and engage in metal manufacturing. Large deposits of copper were available in England in the region around Cornwall. From the early 1700's through the first part of the nineteenth century, Cornwall was the center of English copper production.

Progress in various types of industries took place in England during the eighteenth century. Improvements in mining ores and many innovations in manufacturing occurred which helped to ease and quicken the process of making items from copper and its alloys.

Copper was not an easy metal to extract from its ore. The ore itself was difficult to mine, and once it was brought to the Earth's surface, it had to go through several processes before it was properly refined for use. The ore had to be "dressed," which was done by separating the usable ore from the unusable. Many tons of ore could be mined which actually might produce very little copper. After dressing, the ore was smelted. During the smelting process, arsenic was burned off as a by-product. The fumes were poisonous and hazardous to both workers and the surrounding area. For that reason, smelting plants were located some distance from towns and villages.

Smelted copper was poured into slabs or ingots which could be refired, melted, and worked by hand. The copper was hammered into variable sizes and thickness to make different objects. Some articles were completely beaten or hammered into shape while others were made from separate pieces joined together by soldering. Copper was rarely cast, even though casting was widely used as a method of shaping objects made from copper alloys such as bronze or brass. Copper did not have enough strength to be cast into most items.

During the eighteenth century, it became possible to roll metal into sheets by machines. The sheets could be cut into precise sizes, resulting in more uniformity for shaping articles. Dovetailing was a method used to join sheets of copper. A piece of copper was cut with indentations, and another piece was cut with projections which would fit together. A soldering metal joined the two parts. The soldering metal had to have a lower melting point than copper. Lead, tin, and brass were used. The soldering was visible because of its different color. Pieces might be dovetailed on the side, around the body, or on the base.

Dovetailed joints were originally cut by hand. They were usually large and widely spaced during the 1700's, and the cuts were often irregular. During the nineteenth century, dovetailing became more exact. The metal was notched by machine and a regular pattern was produced. Simple straight seams began to replace dovetail construction during the 1800's.

Another method of shaping metals was introduced during the early 1800's. This was a spinning process where objects were made by using a die and rotating device which produced objects without any seams. The pieces were also much lighter in weight.

In England, in 1769, a procedure was patented for stamping designs on metals. Later, stamp and die techniques were adapted to shaping whole small objects such as hardware. By the beginning of the nineteenth century, larger items could also be shaped entirely by stamping. England's metal industry was, in fact, almost totally mechanized by about 1800.

Other important inventions in connection with copper took place in England during the eighteenth century. Especially notable was a new method of tinning copper. Some foods, in direct contact with copper, created a chemical reaction that resulted in a tainted taste and even food poisoning. Lining pans with tin solved the problem. Tinning prevented the tainted taste, but unfortunately, lead had to be used in that process. Lead was necessary as a flux to make the tin adhere to the copper. Lead, of course, caused a slow form of poisoning. A method of tinning without using lead was sought for many years; it was finally discovered about 1756 (Wills, 1968). During the twentieth century, stainless steel largely has replaced tin for lining copper cooking ware.

Plating copper with another metal was possible after 1742. Thomas Boulsover, working in Sheffield, England, introduced the technique. A sheet of copper was placed between two sheets of silver and heated until the metals fused together. The plated copper was then rolled into thin sheets which could be fashioned into different objects. *Sheffield plate* became the name coined for items made in that manner. Objects had the look of solid silver, but the cost of manufacturing, and hence the cost to the customer, was considerably less. Consequently, another important contribution was added to the long list of uses for copper.

Electroplating replaced Sheffield plating toward the middle of the nineteenth century. That technique of plating one metal with another by means of a chemical process called electrodeposition was discovered by the Elkingtons, another English company. Electroplating was easier and less expensive than Sheffield plating. Not only silver, but gold and other metals have continued to be used to electroplate copper. Today many items which were once electroplated are stripped to the copper base metal. Silver plated pieces show wear over time and are unattractive. Replating is expensive and is not permanent. By stripping away the silver or other metal, a perfectly fine and lasting piece of copper will be uncovered! Businesses throughout the United States specialize in stripping metal today.

There was little American copper manufacturing until after the beginning of the nineteenth century. By English law, American colonies were forbidden to engage in any form of manufacturing in order to provide a ready market for the mother country's goods and also to serve as a source of raw materials. Such laws, of course, were difficult, if not impossible to enforce. Records show that various individuals did work as coppersmiths before independence was won in this country. For the most part, however, the coppersmiths worked with scrap copper rather than imported copper ingots or native copper.

Paul Revere, America's most famous coppersmith, was working with copper in the last quarter of the eighteenth century. He imported copper from England and later developed methods to improve the use of scrap metals. Examples of his work are museum pieces today. After 1800, however, his business focused on commercial and industrial uses of copper for construction.

During the early 1800's, other foreign sources of copper, in addition to those in England, became available, which enabled American copper manufacturing to really grow as an industry. Although copper was available in the colonies, the metal was not mined to any great extent until around the middle 1800's, when vast deposits became available from the western mountain regions. It had always been cheaper to import the metal, and even with large accessible deposits, that has continued to be true even today.

Collecting Copper

There is a large demand for "old" copper of all types. "Old," however, is a relative term. When used in relation to copper available today, the word does not usually imply "ancient," or even several hundred years. Old copper most often refers to pieces made after 1850 until about 1930. Examples from that period are in greater supply. Many items made during that era are also truly relics of the past in the eyes of young collectors, and they are nostalgic memories for many others.

The large shipments of antiques imported from England and other countries for some years now often contain copper. Occasionally, some pieces from the eighteenth century or early nineteenth century are included, but most pieces date from a much later time. When such early copper does surface, the price can be quite out of reach for the majority of collectors. Copper, in general, is much more scarce than other antiques such as furniture, glass, ceramics, or even other metals like brass or silver. Just take a look when browsing at shops, shows, or flea markets, and that fact will be quite clear. Copper enthusiasts must diligently search to find interesting pieces.

"Old copper" brings to mind basically utilitarian articles, simply or even crudely made, with little, if any, decoration. A lot of copper does fit such a description. Highly decorative copper, such as jardinieres, vases, and wall plaques, can be found, however. Many purely functional copper items were also decorated as well.

Pierced or punched patterns and randomly hammered work are perhaps the simplest forms of decoration found on copper. Engraved designs, made by cutting into the metal with a sharp tool, and embossing (repoussé), achieved by hammering designs into the metal from the reverse side, can be quite elaborate. The ability to stamp patterns on sheet metal greatly widened decorating possibilities for machine made pieces, allowing very detailed and intricate decoration. Gilding and enameling also have often been used to decorate copper. Other metals such as silver, pewter, and brass were combined with copper simply because the combination of the two metals was attractive. Some examples of those different decorating techniques will be seen in the photographs.

Decorative copper can reflect definite shapes and designs in vogue during certain historical eras. Pieces may exhibit Georgian lines or Art Nouveau decor, for example. Those periods which are most often used to identify particular styles are:

Arts and Crafts—a movement during the late nineteenth century, circa 1875, emphasizing original designs and hand-crafted construction. The trend was initiated in response to the growth of machine-made, mass produced styles predominant during the middle Victorian years. (For example, see plate 390.)

Art Deco—a style focusing on geometric lines and stylized designs, popular from circa 1925 until 1940. The name comes from the 1925 Paris exhibition, *Exposition des Arts Decoratifs et Industriels Modernes*. (See plate 386.)

Art Nouveau—literally a new form of art, in reaction to elaborate, over-worked Victorian designs. Art Nouveau styles were characterized by smooth flowing lines and naturalistic subjects. The new trend was popular for only a short time, circa 1890 until 1905. (See plate 384.)

Georgian—several styles, marked by a stately, classical line, introduced over a long period, circa 1714 to 1830, when England's kings were all named George (George I through George IV). (See plate 380.)

Victorian—very ornate, rococo styles popular during the reign of Queen Victoria, 1837 to 1901. (See plate 366.)

Among collectors, American-made copper items are highly prized over foreign-made copper. It is difficult to attribute copper articles to specific origins, however. Not only did the early makers in Europe or America seldom mark their wares, but types of objects made and styles of pieces were also quite similar. English manufacturers copied German or other European designs, and Americans, in turn, copied English examples. Moreover, the types of items and the styles did not change very much over time. As a result, dating is rather inexact.

A mark, or a name, on a piece of copper does not necessarily indicate a particular coppersmith. The name or initials may only refer to the owner of the article. It was not uncommon for individuals to have their name engraved on metal wares. The objects were treasured possessions. They were cared for, mended when necessary, and handed down to succeeding generations.

Unless the name on a copper item can be matched to a recorded coppersmith, the manufacturer cannot usually be proved. If a mark includes a location, the country of origin is not difficult to determine. Marks which do not include locations, however, leave the origin uncertain, unless the name can be matched to a known coppersmith of a particular country. Relatively few such names have been recorded, and even they may not have marked all or any of their wares.

One American writer, Henry J. Kauffman, has compiled a list of American coppersmiths and the years during which they worked. He shows approximately 140 names of persons who were known as coppersmiths working between 1740 and 1863 in Connecticut, Maryland, Massachusetts, New York, and Pennsylvania. (See his "Early American Brass and Copper and its makers," pp. 104-107 in Albert Revi (ed.), *Collectible Iron, Tin, Copper & Brass*, 1974). On today's market, however, few pieces surface with one of those signatures. If an old piece does have a mark, it would be worth the time to see if the name does appear on Kauffman's list. It is not impossible for rarities to crop up now and then.

Manufacturer's marks were used more frequently, both here and abroad, after 1900. Thus marked examples from after the turn of the century are more common. They are not considered "rare" in the same sense as eighteenth and early nineteenth century markings. Few pieces illustrated in this book were marked. For the marked pieces, the prices generally reflect their degree of rareness.

Most of the copper featured in this book dates from the last quarter of the nineteenth century through the first quarter of the twentieth century. Dates have not been included in the captions of those photographs. The term *nineteenth century*, however, has been used to indicate a period earlier than the late 1800's; similarly, *twentieth century* has been used to indicate a time later than 1925.

The majority of copper in this survey was also of European or American origin, as opposed to Oriental, Far Eastern, etc. Country of origin has been included in the descriptions of the items where it was reasonably possible to determine. For instance, recent European imports are obviously European rather than American. Some of those are also identifiable as English rather than French, etc., or vice versa. After 1890, United States tariff laws required foreign countries to mark wares exported to America. Therefore, distinguishing American-made copper from European-made copper became less problematic. The inclusion of a country's mark on a piece of copper also signifies that the item was made after 1890.

Current prices for antique copper have been influenced by several factors. The base price of copper increased sharply during the early 1980's. The high price of raw copper encouraged some people to round up their bits and pieces to be sold for scrap. Others began to stash away the metals in all of its forms, including pennies. Some banks even found it necessary to pay a premium if people would cash in their pennies because of the scarcity.

Higher copper prices and the resulting hoarding caused prices to escalate for all types of manufactured copper. That increase was also reflected in the price demanded and paid for old copper. For example, copper wash boilers which sold for $40.00 to $50.00 in the late 1970's can seldom be purchased for less tha[n] $80.00 to $100.00 today. That same type of increas[e] can be seen for numerous other articles of collectibl[e] copper.

A widening interest in kitchen collectibles, prim[i]tives, and tools has caused prices to remain high fo[r] copper. Interior decorators and home decorating publ[i]cations have helped to acquaint the general publi[c] with the warmth and charm old copper furnishes a[s] accents and accessories for any type of home, ultra[-]modern to log cabin style. Warming pans hang by th[e] fireplace, a variety of molds line a kitchen wall, an[d] coal scuttles and preserving pans hold magazines o[r] kindling wood. Today, interest in old copper is by n[o] means confined to antique and metal collectors.

Raw copper prices have stabilized, but prices fo[r] collectible copper items have not decreased. Bargain[s] are hard to find. Late twentieth century American al[l] copper pennies may, in fact, be the most affordable o[f] all copper collectibles. Since 1982 pennies have bee[n] made of zinc and only coated with a layer of copper. I[t] began to cost nearly a penny to make a penny! Ameri[-]can zinc pennies may even become extinct. Englan[d] discontinued minting her coppers several years ag[o] and the same has been suggested for our coin system.

Prices are not likely to decrease for copper in th[e] future. Even mid-twentieth century pieces are attract[-]ing the collector's eye. Now, they are a good bit less i[n] cost than turn of the century items. Many, howeve[r] continue to treasure and search for much older exam[-]ples, finding cost secondary to owning an authenti[c] part of the past.

An unwelcome by-product of mounting interes[t] and high prices for old copper is the rampant deluge o[f] reproductions of a number of antique and collectibl[e] copper items. Through the ages, copper, of course, ha[s] been copied, as have other metals such as silver[,] bronze, pewter, and brass. Copies of seventeenth cen[-]tury pieces were made in the eighteenth century, an[d] eighteenth century copper was copied during the nine[-]teenth century. Those copies have now been around fo[r] quite a number of years. Thus, they have become legit[-]imately "old," meriting their own antique value an[d] interest.

N.H. Moore gives an enlightening account of cop[-]per reproductions made in New York City.

> In Allen Street you will hear the sound of the metal-worker as he swings his mallet, and if you are allowed to penetrate the dusky recesses of the back shop you will find at work a swarthy man with dark eyes, and hanging around him are shears and pinchers, hammers and mallets, sheets of copper and patterns by which to cut out his metal. He works at a long rough table, and near at hand is a crude furnace at which he heats his metal, and when it is at the proper temperature to make it malleable, he begins to hammer it into shape, stroke by stroke. As it slowly takes form you see the graceful shapes you admire growing before your eyes, with the hammer-marks which are always so esteemed

as showing the work to be hand-made rather than machine-made. To suit 'the trade,' some of these newly made goods are battered and dented, and hung in the smoke to darken (p.167).

Do not start looking for this shop. The author was writing around the turn of this century! (N.H. Moore, *Old Pewter, Brass, Copper & Sheffield Plate* (1905), 1933.) No doubt many of those copper items now make up part of today's collectible market. Those new pieces were the concern of Moore in the early 1900's, but today the objects are genuinely old.

Like Moore, today's collector must be concerned with currently made reproductions. Unlike those "new" items made in the early 1900's and described by Moore, today's repros are not handmade. They may be advertised as the "antiques of tomorrow," but I am quite skeptical about whether they will be able to hold up to the test of time as well as those earlier hand-made copper reproductions.

Current copper "repros" should not be confused with other new copper which may be made along traditional or antique lines such as kitchen wares, lighting fixtures, and fireplace equipment. That form of new copper is usually well made, often marked, and sold at various retail outlets such as department stores, hardware shops, or mail order outlets, places where new, rather than old, merchandise is expected to be found.

The repros on the other hand, are sold almost exclusively to the "antique trade" or some other retail business such as gift shops and restaurants specializing in a country store or home-style cooking atmosphere. The repros have been made for several years. They are manufactured in various foreign countries such as Taiwan, Japan, and Korea, and imported to this country by a number of entrepreneurs. The importers advertise the products as reproductions. They sell the pieces at very low wholesale prices in general. Pieces are even marked with the country of origin, but the mark is only a stick-on label, easily removable.

Although the businesses are not misrepresenting their merchandise or pricing items as though they were old, they do restrict their customers to "the trade," that is retailers who, by and large, are antique and collectibles dealers. To purchase from their catalogs or showrooms, dealer identification must be presented. Consequently, where are those new pieces of copper going to be sold? Of course, they are found mostly where one expects to find authentic antiques and collectibles.

From the tremendous business the importing firms conduct, it is apparent that there is a large market for reproductions of all kinds, including copper, as shown by the number and variety of items which are available from those sources. Genuine antiques are getting harder and harder to find as well as more expensive each year. More people are aware of the value of their possessions, and rarely make the mistake of parting with a treasure for a small sum. I surmise that is why many dealers purchase the repros. They help fill in their stock and are easy and inexpensive to buy. Persons wanting a few pieces of copper for decorating a home may go to an antique shop to find it. Because copper is scarce, however, they may not find what they want, or the price may be more than they want to spend, thus they purchase a new repro to achieve the "effect." Because the repros do sell, dealers continue to stock them.

Many dealers handling repros will tell the customer that the copper is new, but some may not. It is not uncommon for new copper to be purchased as old. Prices have a way of edging up each year so that the gap between prices for old copper and new copper narrows some year by year. The price tag is still usually a good indication of whether the article is old or new. With even a hundred percent mark-up, most repros are well below the cost of the same piece made fifty or more years ago. A copper bedwarmer for $25.00, a jelly kettle for $35.00, or a ship's lantern for $27.00 immediately identifies the piece as new, not a "steal."

When in doubt about whether copper is old or new, inspect objects carefully. Look for the patina on unlacquered pieces. If the copper has been lacquered, ask the dealer when the finish was applied. Many dealers have all of their old copper lacquered because some people prefer it. If the dealer can only tell you that the piece was lacquered when purchased, then it is indeed possible that the item is new. New coal hods, umbrella stands, bedwarmers and tea kettles have a lacquered finish. Some of the cooking ware does not, however. The reproduction kitchen wares, however, are not tin lined.

Repros are usually much lighter in weight than old copper. Some new pieces, such as lamps, may be weighted with lead. Copper is rolled very thinly for constructing the cheap imports. Edges are sharp, and pieces may not be finished off very well. New copper dents easily. "Distressing" is not uncommon, but it is usually so overdone that it is easily recognized as a ploy to make an item look authentically worn.

Dovetailed construction is really too expensive to be copied. Simple seams should not show an overabundance of soldering metal. Copper repros may have a tin colored soldering abundantly dripping out of the seams. Another trick to "age" copper is an applied blue-green color randomly dappled on items such as weathervanes. The color is supposed to resemble the verdigris copper acquires through exposure to the weather. Some new pieces, which would never have been exposed to the elements originally, also have this coating!

Handles and feet on copper reproductions strive to copy those used years ago. Old iron handles may be attached to new pieces, or new iron handles with a fake "rusting" can be added. Brass paw feet, and handles, fashioned with lion heads and a ring through the nose, are commonly seen on a number of repros. The ceramic "delft-style" handle on a variety of copper coal buckets is a mark that the piece is not very old. Some of those new buckets have been around for several years now, but they are still being made.

Beware of marks found on some copper items. Identifying names are added so that articles may look as though they were made for certain businesses such as a hotel or railroad, or that they were made by a specific firm. The names are merely decorative. Markings embossed in large letters should not be difficult to determine as new. A copper and brass spittoon with "Wells Fargo" on the front is just one example. Other names stamped on small brass plates and attached to items such as bedwarmers and lanterns can cause more confusion.

Current copper reproductions may not even be made entirely of copper. Three different dealers showed me the same candy mold as an example of "old" copper. The piece is new and only copper plated iron. Be sure to take along a magnet when searching for copper. It can be very handy!

A few of the most common copper repros are shown at the end of the book. Hopefully they will help warn collectors about the types of new items which may crop up at various antique locations today. In addition, they should serve as a record which will alert future collectors to the copper reproductions made during the 1980's. In a few years, such items will have begun to acquire their own "patina" from handling, dust, and dents, as well as prices closer to those asked for the real thing!

Useful Terms

Several different names are often encountered for the same copper objects; and the same name is frequently used for two or more objects. Some similar cooking items often have very different names. This is true especially for kitchen related wares. A pan is not just a pan, for example. It may be a cauldron, a preserving pan, or a sauce pan. Names for articles have evolved through time based on how the piece was generally used. The same type of objects could have been used for different purposes in different countries or by different groups of people in the same country. Thus, it is not uncommon for more than one word to be found for similar items. Pails and buckets are basically the same object and so are skillets and frying pans.

Sometimes names have strayed away from the intended purpose of the piece. A tea kettle is actually any type of kettle used to boil water or any other liquid. Tea is not made in the kettle, and the kettle's purpose is not limited to boiling water for tea. "Kettle" originally meant any large, deep pan used for cooking over a fire. When the custom of drinking tea was introduced, *tea kettle*, a word for an entirely different type of object, identified its purpose. *Kettle*, however, is still used to identify either one.

Some of those confusing names for copper objects are described here. Other words whose meaning might not be clear and which have been used to describe some of the copper illustrated are also included. The number in parentheses at the end of the description refers to the photograph number of one example of that item.

Basin—a bowl, more shallow than a tub, for washing hands, laundry, etc. (607)

Bed Warmer—a metal container, round or oval shaped, with a small neck and lid. The containers were filled with hot water and placed in the bed. They are later than Warming Pans. (594)

Chamberstick—a candle holder with a large flat base and attached handle. They were designed for lighting the way to bed. (588)

Cistern—a water container, usually covered, equipped with a spigot. (600)

Cauldron—a large kettle. (457)

Can—a tall, cylinder-shaped container with a narrow neck. (497)

Coal Box—basically any covered coal container. (376)

Coal Carrier—a covered pan with a long handle. They were made to carry hot coals from one fireplace or stove to another. The top may have punched holes. They can be confused with Warming Pans. (430)

Coal Scuttle—a coal container usually having part of the top covered. They may have a ring attached at the back for holding a small shovel or scoop. (372)

Colander—a round pan, pierced over all or most of the bottom, for draining liquids from foods. (435)

Fender—a horizontal piece of metal, only several inches in height, placed along the length of a fireplace to hold back the ashes. (373)

Geyser—a gas-powered hot water heater. (606)

Jardiniere—the French term for a planter and stand. The pot alone, however, is often referred to as a jardiniere. (367)

Jug—a fat, round pitcher; or a cylinder-shaped container with a small neck and handle. (502)

Kettle—a utensil for boiling foods or liquids. Kettles are deep, and they are larger than Sauce Pans. Handles may be attached to the side, or across the top (bail-type). Except for Tea Kettles, most are shaped similarly, but sizes vary greatly. Early ones were used for cooking over an open fire, and later ones were used on top of the stove, rather than in an oven. A few varieties are listed here:
Apple Butter Kettle—a very large kettle for making preserves, usually unlined. (446)
Fish Kettle—an oval-shaped pan for cooking fish, usually has an insert and a lid. (512)
Jelly Kettle—similar to a Preserving Kettle, but shaped like a pail. (452)
Preserving Kettle—any kettle for making preserves, often called a Preserving Pan. (445)
Stewing Kettle—similar to a Preserving Kettle, usually tin lined. (454)
Tea Kettle—a utensil with a spout, handle, and a lid, for boiling water. (537)

Lantern—an enclosed lighting fixture which may be suspended or carried. (364)

Lavabo—a basin for washing hands, usually placed below a wall-mounted cistern. (599)

Log Container—a large open container for holding logs. They may be highly decorated. Some look similar to large planters, and they are often sold today as such. (380)

Loving Cup—an oversized cup, originally intended for ceremonial purposes where the cup was passed around, and each person sipped (wine) from it. Through time, its use has evolved to a form of trophy. They may have several handles. (405)

Measures—usually cup or pitcher-shaped, often marked to indicate specific amounts. Hot Liquid Measures have long handles. (465, 464)

Molds—used to shape food into various forms and sizes, primarily used for eye-appeal. They range from simple to quite elaborate in design. Similar looking molds are referred to as Jelly Molds, Pudding Molds, Vegetable Molds, or Cake Molds. They can be used for any of those types of foods. *Jelly Mold*, however, refers to any mold used for a gelatin-based mixture; it does not necessarily mean a breakfast jelly. Candy or Chocolate Molds are made in the form of a pan with small individual shapes for forming pieces of candy. Cake Molds often have a center tube, and they are deeper than a cake pan. (471, 478)

Pail—a cylinder-shaped container with a bail handle, no lid, similar to a bucket. (462)

Pans—a broad term applied to a number of different types of cooking utensils.
Baking Pan—any rather shallow pan used in the oven. Cake and bread pans usually do not have handles; roasting pans do. (528)
Candy Pan—a large round pan with side handles. They are not as deep as Preserving Kettles, but they are sometimes referred to as Preserving Pans or Kettles. (444)
Ebleskiver Pan—a pan with several cup shapes in the bottom. These are for making Danish dessert dumplings. Ebleskiver Pans are often confused with Escargot Pans. (525)
Escargot Pans—similar to Ebleskiver Pans, except the cups are smaller. (527)
Frying Pan—a round, rather shallow pan with a long, straight handle, designed for cooking over a flame, or on top of a stove. (524)
Preserving Pan—the same as a Preserving Kettle.
Roasting Pan—a deep pan for cooking meats in the oven. (529)
Sauce Pan—a deep, round pan with a long handle and a lid. Sizes vary, and the pans were used for cooking any food that needed to boil or simmer. (514)
Stewing Pan—the same as Stewing Kettle.

Peat Bucket—an open container for holding blocks of peat or turf used in building a fire, similar to a coal bucket. (379)

Pitcher—a cylinder-shaped container for liquids, having a spout and a cup-style handle. Sizes vary from small cream pitchers to large ale tankards. (500)

Planter—any deep receptacle for holding a plant. Originally, the containers were designed for actual planting, but today the term commonly refers to a decorative holder for clay-potted plants. Planter and Jardiniere are used interchangeably. (391)

Plaque—a decorative dish designed for hanging. They are often called Chargers. (398)

Plate Warmer—a shallow pan fitted with a plate or platter on top. The pan has a small opening which can be filled with hot water. (567)

Pots—a broad term, like Pans, applied to a number of cooking vessels. "Pot" or "Pan" often refers to the same object. Pots are deeper than pans.
Coffee Pot—pitcher-shaped with either a short open spout, or a long narrow spout. Sometimes the short spouts may have a hinged lid cover. (416) Percolator Coffee Pots often have a glass knob on top. (421)
Stock Pot—a large, deep, cylinder-shaped container with or without a lid, side handles. It may have a spigot. (505, 506)
Tea Pot—usually shorter than a coffee pot, with a long spout, handle, and lid, used for brewing tea. (563)

Samovar—a large covered container, equipped with a spigot and some form of heating to keep the beverage warm; similar to an Urn. (564)

Sconce—a wall-mounted light fixture. (361)

Skimmer—a utensil for separating one substance from another; sizes vary; some are finely pierced all over, like a sieve or filter for separating milk; others may be in the form of a flat bowled ladle for separating solid substances, like fat, from a broth or stew; another type has a pierced bowl. (439, 443, 442)

Skillet—a Frying Pan. (Originally, the skillet was a three-legged pot with a long handle, made for cooking over an open fire.) (524)

Steamer—a fairly deep pot with a lid. They may have a tray to hold the food above the water. For steaming, only a small amount of water is used, in order to cook the food quickly to a just-tender consistency. (509)

Tea Kettle—see Kettles.

Tinder Box—a round cup-shaped container used for starting a fire. Pieces of charred cloth, flint, and steel were kept in the box. A lid, made with a candleholder, fitted on top. Once the fire was ignited, the candle could be lighted and placed in the holder. (436) *Tinder Box* may also refer to larger containers for holding pieces of kindling material. (373)

Tub—any large, deep container used for bathing or laundry. (612)

Urn—a large, covered container for serving hot liquids, equipped with a spout and some means of heating. Early ones had spirit lamps; later ones use canned heat, or electricity. (Urn also refers to a covered vase for holding the ashes of the cremated.) (564)

Warming Pan—a covered pan with a long iron or wooden handle. The pan was filled with hot coals to warm the bed before retiring. Some pans have pierced tops. They are commonly called Bed Warmers. (590)

Wash Boiler—an oval-shaped tub for washing clothes or boiling water. It may have a lid. (615, 619)

Antique Brass

PLATE 3. Candleholder, 7"h, 6½"d, French, ornate styling in scroll work connecting top of holder to base. The base rests on three rounded feet, one of a pair.

PLATE 4. Candleholder, 47"h. This is a floor-style or altar type holder often used in churches. The candle rests on the spike which is called a "pricket." The pricket style is one of the earliest forms of candleholders. This example is French circa early 1800's. Note the paw feet and applied cherubs at the base.

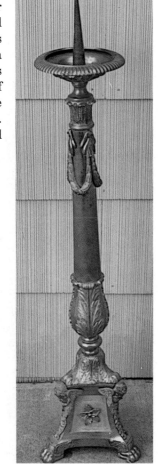

PLATE 1. Candleholder, 7"h, 2½"d of octagonal sided base, English, circa mid 1800's, one of a pair.

PLATE 2. Chamberstick, 7¼" l, heart shaped, English. Chambersticks were carried to light the way to bed or up the stairs. Many were simply round and made of other material as well as brass.

PLATE 5. Candleholder, 35½"h. This is an institutional or altar type candleholder, originally half cast and held together by a central iron rod which also forms the base of the interior socket. Note the different components of the overall design, English or American, circa mid 1800's.

PLATE 8. Candleholder, 8"h, 3½" base, inverted baluster stem, English, mid 1800's, one of a pair.

PLATE 6. Candlestick, 7¼"h, Queen Anne period, circa 1710, the seam is faintly visible down the side, the base is octagonal with deeply notched corners.

PLATE 7. Candleholder, 10"h, base is 4½" x 3½", English, early 1800's, one of a pair.

PLATE 9. Candleholder, 9½"h, 4"d base, English, mid 1800's.

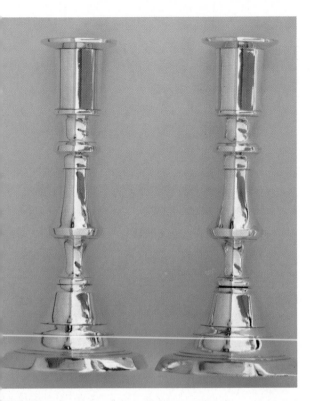

PLATE 10. Pair of Candleholders, 6"h, octagonal bases, 2¾"d, equipped with push-up ejectors, circa mid 1800's.

PLATE 11. Pair of Candleholders, 9¾"h bases, 3½" sq, beehive and diamond design, equipped with push rods and brass ejector buttons, marked "England," circa early 1890's.

PLATE 12. Pair of Candleholders, 8½"h, octagonal bases, baluster design with push-up ejectors, Victorian, circa mid 1800's.

PLATE 13. The assortment of candleholders in photographs 13 and 14 are salesmen's samples. Pair of candleholders with hexagon sided bases, 3½"h; two light holder, 2½"h.

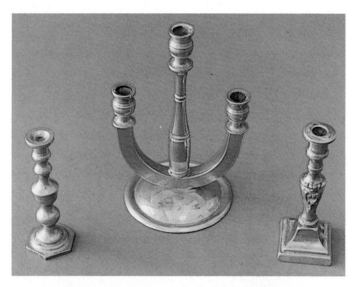

PLATE 14. Candleholders, salesmen's samples. The holder on the left with hexagon sided base is 3½"h; right with square base, 3½"h; three-light candelabrum, center, 4½"h.

PLATE 17. Candleholder, 6½"h, base, 5"sq, ornate design featuring *fleur de lis* with winged griffins flanking the socket, probably French, circa mid to late 1800's.

PLATE 18. Candleholders in a "barley twist" design, marked "Made in England."

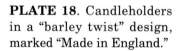

PLATE 15. Candleholders, 8"h, deep drip pan below nozzle of holder.

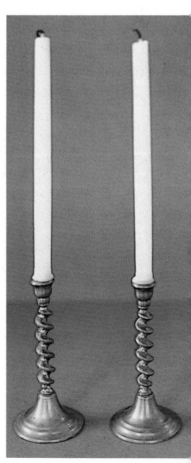

PLATE 16. Candleholders, 10"h, American, 18th century. These holders are equipped with push-ups, which were bars inserted in the stems which could be "pushed-up" to eject the candle stub after it had burned down.

PLATE 20. Photographs 20 through 26 are examples of Wall Sconces. This type of lighting has been popular for centuries. Sconces were originally made of wood and then iron, mounted on walls to hold candles and furnish light. During the 20th century wall sconces were wired for electricity and equipped with "false" candleholders to hold light bulbs which are often shaped in the form of a flame. The Wall Sconce in this photograph is very rococo in design and features a mirror in the center, English, Victorian, one of a pair, 18½"l, 13"w.

LATE 19. Pair of Peg Lamps, rench, enameled glass bases, set n a pair of square based brass andleholders. The Peg Lamp is a carce item. The glass font burned il and was made with an exten-ion on the base to fit into the andleholder, circa early to mid 800's.

PLATE 21. Wall Sconce, 15"w, 19"l, heavily embossed designs featuring a bird and scenic decor, English.

PLATE 22. Electrified Wall Sconce, 1"l, circa 1920's, one of a pair.

PLATE 23. Wall Sconce, 26"l, 18"w, form of "Medusa" in high relief, English, circa 1830.

PLATE 24. Wall Sconce, 9¾"h, 4⅝"w, hand hammered work featuring an Art Nouveau repoussé design of cockatoos and flowers on a stippled background.

PLATE 26. Wall Sconces, 10½"h, sheet copper with hand hammered floral designs mounted on oak with a carved design of oak leaves and acorns, European, probably Bavarian, circa late 1800's.

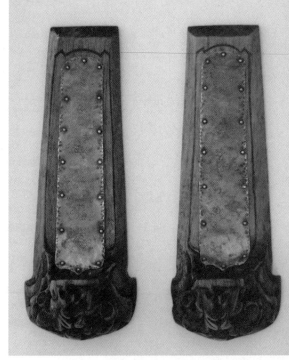

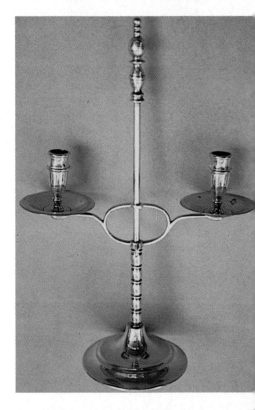

PLATE 25. Wall Sconce, 11½"h; the two sockets are separated by a small cup type match holder, American, circa first quarter of the 20th century.

PLATE 27. Candelabra (Candelabrum indicates only one) were designed to provid more light at the table and thus vary in th number of candles they hold. They wer originally made in pairs, but often only on remains of that pair today. Because dinin tables are not as large, however, one is ofte sufficient and can be used on many othe pieces of furniture as well such as pianos desks, and mantels for example. The one i this photograph is one of a pair, 16"h, 10"w a simple but elegant design, English.

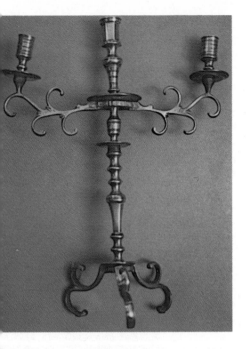

PLATE 28. Candelabrum, 20"h, 16"w, 3 light, English, circa mid 1800's.

PLATE 29. Candelabrum, 4 light, marked "P" in a triangle and made by Pairpoint Manufacturing Co. (New Bedford, Mass.), early 1900's. This item was originally silver plated. Engraved floral design on center stem with "torch flame" finial.

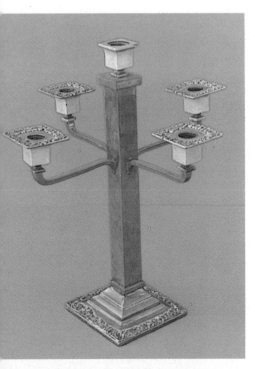

PLATE 30. Candelabrum, 16"h, 5 light, embossed floral designs on base and drip pans, Art Deco style, circa 1930's, originally silver plated.

PLATE 31. Campaign Torch, 15"h (mounted on wooden stand for display). This type of torch was carried by hand in parades during the latter part of the 19th century. It has a spring device inside the stem which pushes up the candle as it burns down. The glass shade (on the side) covers the candle fitting into the socket at the top. These are sometimes mounted on walls today inside or outside the home as unique forms of lighting.

PLATE 33. Kerosene Lamp, 10"h, new satin glass shade.

PLATE 32. Candelabrum, 12"h, 5 light, Art Nouveau style, one of a pair.

PLATE 35. Aladdin Lamp Base, marked "Mantel Lamp Co., Chicago, Made in U.S.A.," 12½"h. Many of these lamps were nickel plated and today have been stripped to the base metal of brass or copper. Price increases if lamp has original shade.

PLATE 34. Kerosene Lamp, 20"h overall, marked "Rayo" American, ca. late 1800's (new shade).

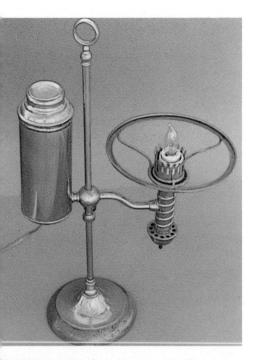

PLATE 36. Student Lamp, 20½"h, reser-
oir for oil on the side. The reservoir and
nt slide up and down to adjust the height
f the light. This one has been electrified
nd lacquered.

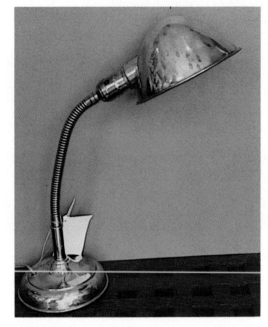

PLATE 37. Goose-Neck Lamp, electric.
The neck bends to direct the light.

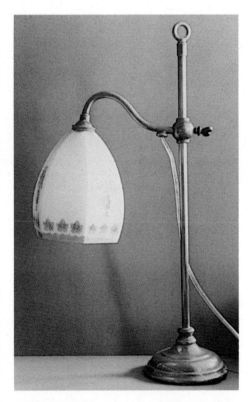

PLATE 38. Desk Lamp, 20"h, electric,
art glass shade, neck adjusts by key.
The art glass shade increases the price
of this lamp.

PLATE 39. Student or Desk Lamp, 17½"h overall, black
metal shade on cast brass body, American, circa 1920's.

PLATE 40. Clamp Lamp, marked "Adjusto-Lite, a Farberware Product, USA and Foreign Patents, July 14, 1914." This type of lamp was quite versatile and could be hung on a wall, placed upright on a desk, or clamped to a surface.

PLATE 41. Table Lamp, electric, 17"h, ornate design of dragon body with lady's head, original silk shade, English, circa 1920's.

PLATE 42. Table Lamp with slag glass inserts in brass shade, silk fringe, Art Deco style, electric.

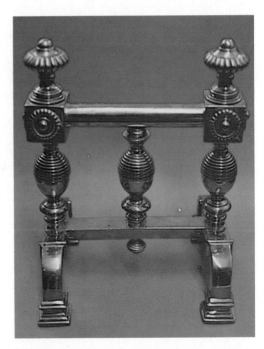

PLATE 43. Fire Dogs are shown in photographs 43 through 46. These are a type of andiron where the logs were laid across the pair. Some were simple and others quite ornate. The ones in this photo are a combination of brass and iron, "l, 5"h, English, circa mid 1800's.

PLATE 44. Fire Dogs, 7"h, 8½"l, European origin.

PLATE 45. Fire Dogs, 8"h, spherical base with embossed flower and leaf designs, European, circa mid 1800's.

PLATE 46. Fire Dog (one of a pair), 11½"h, 8½"w, European, early 1800's.

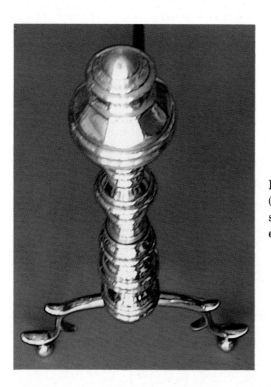

PLATE 47. Andiron (one of a pair), double spur legs, ball feet, early 1800's.

PLATE 48. Pair of Andirons, 18½"h, double spur legs, ball feet, cannonball style, American.

PLATE 49. Brass and Iron Andirons, ornate pierced base with ball feet and finials, note ball finial behind shaft.

PLATE 50. Andirons, French, gilded, "Genie's Lamps with flares" distinguish this pair.

PLATE 51. Pair of Andirons, 19"h, base, 8¼"w, baluster design on cabriole base with a screw-on steeple type finial.

PLATE 52. Fire Back, 28½"h, 18"w, sheet brass with applied decoration, English, circa mid to late 1800's.

PLATE 53. Fire Back, 18½"l, 17½"w, Georgian style, English, circa 1870, intricate cutout work featuring flowers, birds, leaves and a large sunburst at base.

PLATE 54. Fire Back, masted ship in relief decor, English. This type of fire back is typical of the ones made during the 1930's through the 1950's.

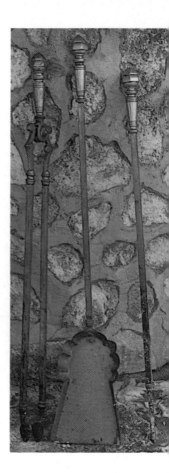

PLATE 56. Fireplace Tools: Shovel, 27"l, Poker, 25"l, Tongs, 26"l.

PLATE 55. Trivet designed to hang on inside of a Fender. The purpose of the trivet was to keep a kettle or pan hot over the fire, English early 1800's.

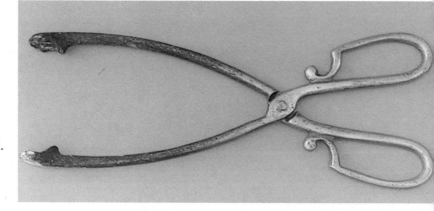

PLATE 57. Brass Coal Tongs, 10½"l.

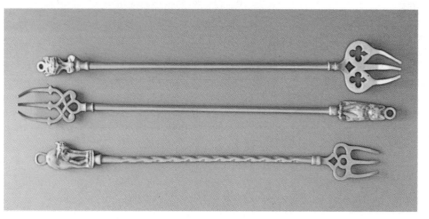

PLATE 58. Toasting Forks, 18" to 20" long with different pierced designs, all with figural cat handles, noted to be marshmallow toasting forks.

PLATE 59. Fender, 24"l, English. Fenders were made to retain the ashes within the fireplace. This one has an attractively simple double row of pierced work for decoration.

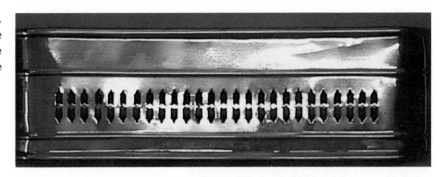

PLATE 60. Photographs 60 through 65 are various containers for coal. They may be called by several names such as coal bucket, coal scuttle or coal hod. The one in this photograph is 8"h, 14"d, English.

PLATE 61. Brass Coal Hod with copper liner, 22"h, English, early to mid 1800's, pattern of punched designs on front and sides, applied handles, footed with embossed designs. The ring visible at the back is to hold the coal shovel.

PLATE 62. Coal Bucket, embossed floral and fruit designs in high relief, English, mid to late 1800's. This piece has been worn completely through in small places around the base.

PLATE 63. Coal Bucket, 13"h, English.

PLATE 65. Coal Scuttle, 14"h, 20"d, similar to one in Photograph 64, but much larger.

PLATE 64. Coal Scuttle, 7"h, 11"d, English.

PLATE 66. Brass Box equipped with casters, English, known as a "Slipper Box." These boxes are often used to store kindling wood by the fireplace today. The examples shown here and in the next photograph were made during the first half of the 20th century, but new ones with similar designs are currently on the market.

PLATE 67. Slipper Box, 14"h, 16½"l, 11"d, mounted on casters, embossed figural tavern scene.

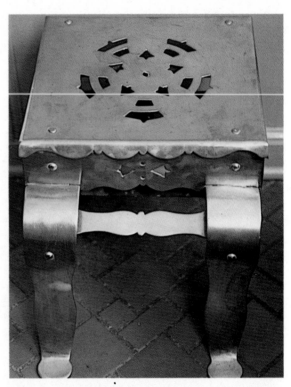

PLATE 69. Footman, 14½"h, 13"w. This example is much larger than the preceding one, English, early to mid 1800's.

PLATE 68. Photographs 68 through 73 are called Footmen or Trivets. Properly speaking, trivets have 3 legs while footmen have four legs. The trivet or footman was made for the fireplace to keep kettles or pans warm. The one in this photograph is 4½"h, 6"l with cut-out club and star shapes and heavy legs, English, ca. mid 1800's.

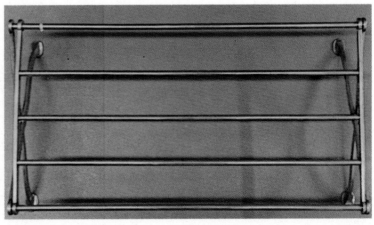

PLATE 70. Folding Fireplace Trivet, 7½"h, 24"l. This one could hold many kettles or pans, and was convenient to store when not in use.

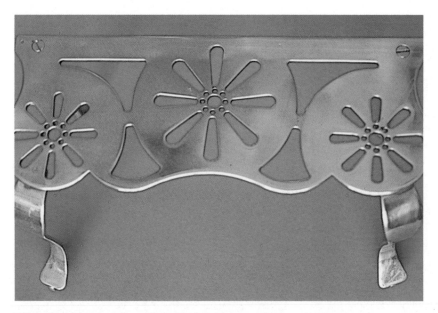

PLATE 71. Footman, 7"h, 16"l, back legs are new, English.

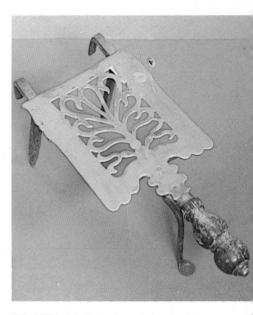

PLATE 72. Trivet on 3 legged iron stand, wooden handle, 11½"l, 5¼"w, early 1800's, English.

PLATE 73. Footman on wrought iron stand, 15½"h, 14"w, solid sheet of brass with no piercing.

PLATE 74. Bed Warmers were extremely useful in the past. They were filled with hot coals and passed back and forth under the bed covers (hence the long handle). This one is 45"l, pan is 12"d with pierced design, English.

PLATE 75. Bed Warmer with copper bottom and brass top, pierced design, New England origin, mid to late 1800's, 41"l, 13"d.

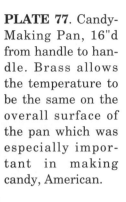

PLATE 77. Candy-Making Pan, 16"d from handle to handle. Brass allows the temperature to be the same on the overall surface of the pan which was especially important in making candy, American.

PLATE 76. Servant's Bell, 13"l, English, early to mid 1800's. This type of bell was rung by a cord connected by a wire to various rooms in the house. A set of these was used "below stairs" and would ring when the cord was pulled "upstairs." Each bell had a different sound.

PLATE 78. Kettle or cauldron 12"h, 19"d, iron bail, American, mid 1800's. This type was used for making apple butter.

PLATE 79. Brass Kettle for making jelly, iron bail, 7"h, 13"d, American, mid to late 1800's.

45

PLATE 80. Kettle, iron handle, English, tin lined, 18th century, decorated with embossed lions and shields. Notice the wear inside the kettle. The piece also has patch marks.

PLATE 81. Milk or Water Pail, 9"h, 10"d. Rim forms loops to hold bail.

PLATE 82. Kettle, 11"h, 9½"d, brass bail.

PLATE 83. Kettle for making jelly or preserves, 7"h, 12½"d, brass handle, American. This style is being copied today.

PLATE 84. Apple Butter Kettle, 10"h, 17"w, iron handle, American, note wear and mending on piece at bottom.

PLATE 85. Butter Mold of wood and brass, 6"h, 9¼"w, American, probably Minnesota or Wisconsin origin, a one pound mold.

PLATE 86. Butter Mold similar to the one in Plate 85.

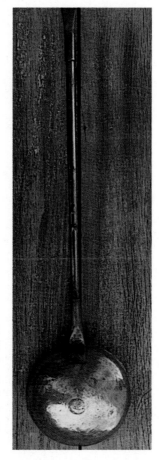

PLATE 87. Dipper, copper bowl with brass handle, another example of brass combined with another material. Brass handles are often found on copper pieces because they do not get hot as quickly as a copper handle. This dipper is 26"l, the bowl is 7½"d, mid to late 1800's.

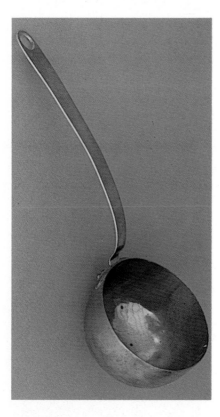

PLATE 88. Dipper, all brass, 13"l, 4½"d bowl.

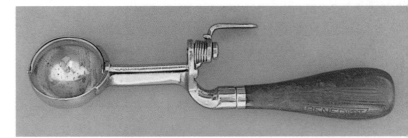

PLATE 90. Ice Cream Dipper, 10"l, brass and wood handle, bowl was nickel plated, some wear showing. Piece is marked "#6 and INDESTRUCTO."

PLATE 91. Ice Cream Dipper, 10"l, brass handle with nickel plated bowl, marked "Gilchrist."

PLATE 89. Ladle, 15"l, pierced to hang, American, circa late 1800's.

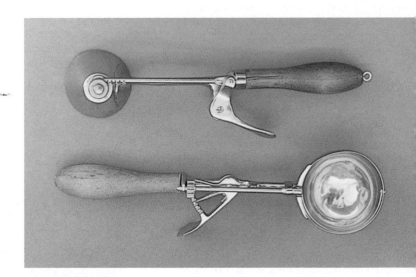

PLATE 92. Two Ice Cream Dippers by Gilchrist. The one at the top is made of brass, nickel, and wood. This particular shape formed "conettes." It is 10½"l, and marked "#33" along with the manufacturer's name. The one at the bottom is 12"l with a wooden handle. All of the original nickel plating has been stripped from the bowl.

PLATE 93. Mug, 7"h, base has been mended with copper.

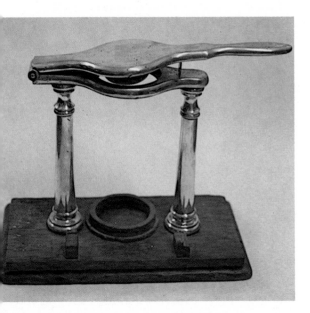

PLATE 94. Lemon Press mounted on wooden stand, English, circa mid 1800's.

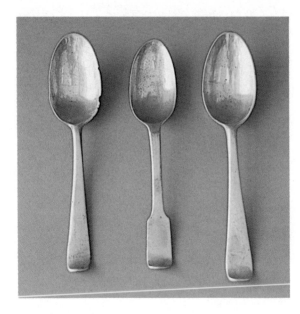

PLATE 95. Three examples of brass teaspoons, quite worn, American, 19th century.

PLATE 96. Mortar, 3¼"h, 5½"d; Pestle, 7"l. These were used in the kitchen for grinding herbs.

PLATE 97. Colander, brass pan with four circular punched designs, iron handle.

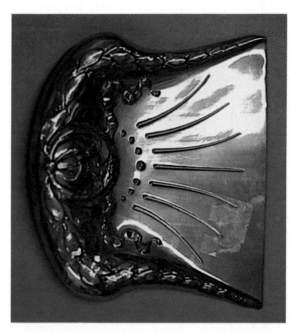

PLATE 98. Dust pan, 8½"l, 8"w, embossed designs, English.

PLATE 99. Food Grinder, 7½"l, brass and cast iron, marked "Standard Werk," circa late 1800's.

PLATE 100. Food Grinder, 7½"l, brass and cast iron, marked "Gesch," circa late 1800's.

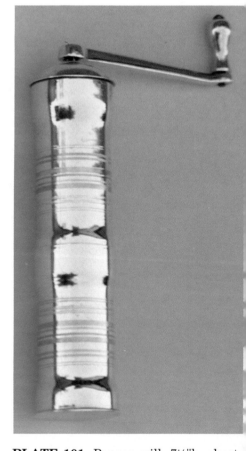

PLATE 101. Pepper mill, 7½"h, sheet-brass body with cast brass crank, German, marked with a stag's head logo and name of manufacturer (illegible), circa late 1800's to early 1900's.

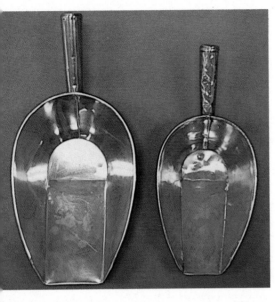

PLATE 102. Scoops for sugar or grain. These are marked "Patented Dec. 8, 1868" on handle, American.

PLATE 103. Tea Caddies, 8"h with copper labels. The one on the left is marked "Tea, Fine Sinagar," and the one on the right "Tea, Choice Assam," English.

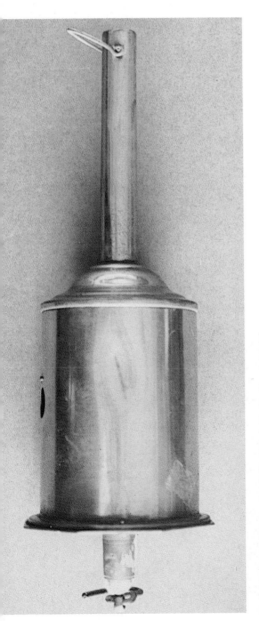

PLATE 105. Rub Boards were essential in the home around the turn of the century. The manufacturer's name is still often visible at the top of many, although it has been worn away on this example. Rub boards of this type were selling for 33 cents in 1908.

PLATE 104. Clockwork Roasting Jack, 11"l, marked "SALTER," English. Roasting devices of this type were made during the early 1800's to cook meat in the fireplace. They were operated by inserting a key into the hole on the side which wound up a spring inside. The spring mechanism was similar to that used in clocks, and thus the name "Clockwork" became identified with the jack. "Bottle-Jack" is also a term used to describe the jack because the spring inside was shaped like a bottle.

51

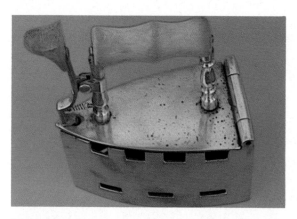

PLATE 106. Charcoal Iron, 8" h, hinged top, wooden handle has been replaced. Variations of this type of iron were used in 19th century and early 20th century American households. Hot coals were placed inside the iron.

PLATE 107. Flat Iron, 6½"l, wooden handle lever opens end to fill with coal, includes separate resting pad.

PLATE 108. Brass Kettle with copper spout 10"h, 12"d, English.

PLATE 109. Kettle, 12" h, goose-neck spout, rounded brass handle.

PLATE 110. Kettle, 8"h, wooden handle and finial. This kettle is early 20th century while the preceding ones are from the 19th century.

PLATE 111. Watering Can, 8"h, 11"w, hinged lid, European.

PLATE 112. Tea Pot with stand and burner, marked "SAS" in a circle, early 1800's.

PLATE 113. Tea Pot, rounded body, wood and brass handle, with 3-legged stand or trivet, English, early 1800's.

PLATE 114. Tea Pot, footed, amber glass handle, English, circa mid 1800's.

PLATE 116. Coffee Service, Art Deco style, circa 1930's marked "Doryln Silversmith."

PLATE 115. Spirit Lamp, 1½"h, 4½"d, repaired on top. This type of lamp burned alcohol and served as a fire to warm dishes, marked "Birmingham, England," maker's name illegible, circa mid to late 1800's.

PLATE 117. Coffee Service, brass with copper hinges on lids, unmarked, Arts and Crafts influence, circa early 1900's, American: Tray, 21"l; Coffee Pot, 8½"h, Covered Creamer, 5"h; Covered Sugar, 5½"h.

PLATE 118. Coffee Pot, Dragon Eye spout, names are engraved on each side, "CARAPLE" and "AMALIE," circa early 20th century.

PLATE 119. Samovar, 25"h overall, marked "Tehran."

PLATE 120. Knife Box or Tray, English, Georgian period, early 1800's, claw feet and pierced designs.

PLATE 121. Wine Cooler on pedestal base, 10"h, 8"d, applied handles of lion heads with rings though noses, mid 20th century.

PLATE 122. Crumber for cleaning the table. These usually had a matching tray.

PLATE 123. Crumber Tray and Holder.

PLATE 124. Creamer and Sugar, brass with pewter handles.

PLATE 125. Tray, 12"d, American, marked "S. & S. H.," originally silver plated, mid 20th century.

PLATE 126. Tray, 11"x16", stippled design, mid 20th century.

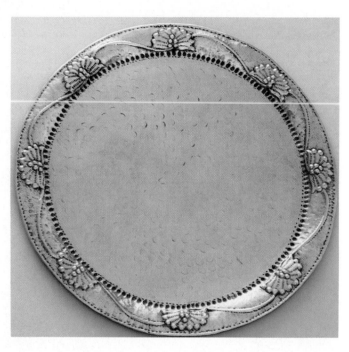

PLATE 127. Charger, 18"d, hand hammered design in an Art Nouveau style, marked with the impressed initials of "JP" in a dotted oval cartouche. Attributed to John Pearson, member of the Guild of Handicraft who worked in metal in Cornwall, England around 1900 during the Arts & Crafts era.

PLATE 128. Salver (or Tray), 12"x9" oval shape, repoussé armorial design, marked "England" with illegible maker's mark, circa late 1800's.

PLATE 129. Tray, 10"d, embossed scroll and floral border design.

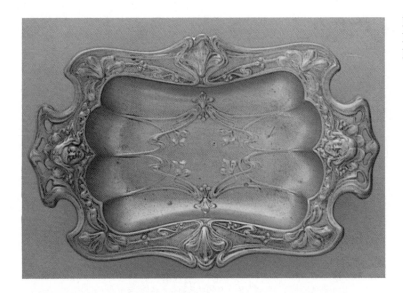

PLATE 130. Tray, 14"l, 9"d, Art Nouveau design in relief, pierced handles.

PLATE 133. Bowl, 10"d, engraved floral and lea designs, marked "China."

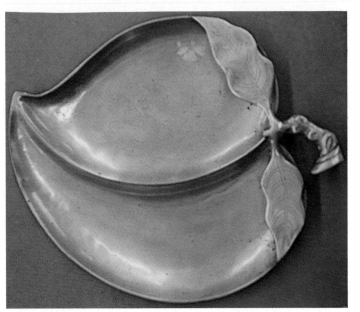

PLATE 131. Tray, fruit shaped, 9"l, marked "Hong Kong," circa mid 20th century.

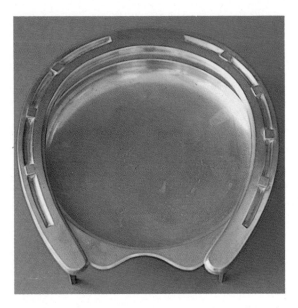

PLATE 132. Tray in horseshoe shape, 10½"l, 7"w, footed, circa mid 20th century.

PLATE 134. Compote, 7"h, 9½"d with figural co per insert of allegorical figures, French, 19th ce tury.

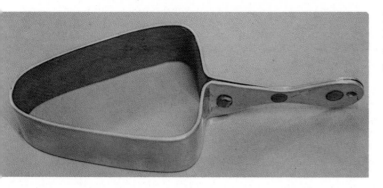

PLATE 135. Trivet, 10"l, 3¼"wide, hollow center. This style of trivet could be used to hold an iron or used at the table for hot dishes.

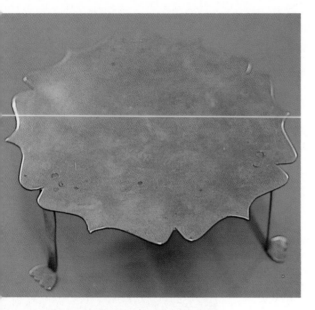

PLATE 136. Trivet, 3½"h, 8"d, fancy scalloped border, smooth top, early 1800's.

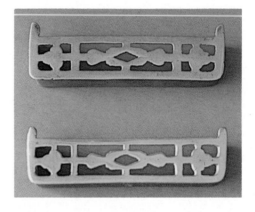

PLATE 138. Salesman's Sample of a Trivet which does not have legs, but rests on a solid strip of metal on three sides. Note the similarity of design to the one in Plate 139.

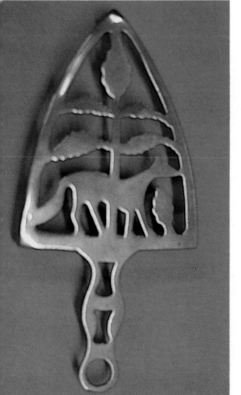

PLATE 139. Trivet, 12"l, 4"w, English.

PLATE 137. Trivet, 7¼"l, fox and tree design.

PLATE 140. Trivet, 1½"h, 7" sq., sheet brass with a repoussé design accented by a hand stippled background, English Arts & Crafts era, circa late 1800's to early 1900's.

PLATE 141. Trivet on pedestal stand, 9½"h, 7"d, the cut-out design is more simple on this trivet than the one in Plate 142, some wear on top.

PLATE 142. Trivet, 9¼"h, 9"sq., elaborate pierced work, English, circa mid 1800's.

PLATE 144. School Bell, 12"h overall, wooden handle. Many reproductions of school bells are made today.

PLATE 145. School Bell, 6"h.

PLATE 143. All types of brass bells are very popular collectibles. Although they served a useful purpose in the past, most are rarely "rung" today! The hand bell in this photograph is English and has been lacquered.

PLATE 146. Call Bell for table, store, or hotel desks.

PLATE 147. Photographs 147 through 152 are of objects connected with various vehicles. Coach lantern, 18"l, mid 1800's.

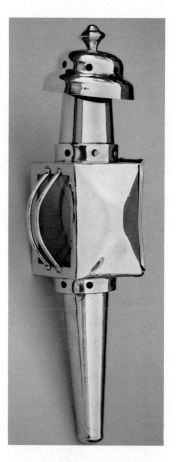

PLATE 148. Coach Lantern, 15½"h, hand made from sheet brass featuring travel guards over the glass (burner is missing), circa mid to late 1800's.

PLATE 149. Rear View Mirror for an early automobile, 8"x10", beveled glass.

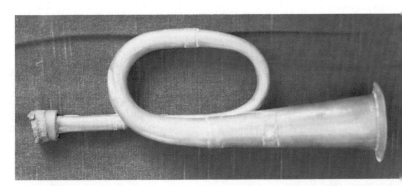

PLATE 152. Brass Car Horn, 12"l, similar to one in preceding photograph, but the rubber pump is missing.

PLATE 150. Car Horn for a DIXIE Model T, 9½"l, 6"d, marked "1872 Edwards, Patent Pending," American.

PLATE 153. Truck Tire Air Gauge, marked "A. Schrader's Son, Service Tire Gauge Division of Scovill Manufacturing Co., Brooklyn, N.Y."

PLATE 151. Brass Car Horn, 18"l, activated by the rubber pump on the end, American, circa late 1800's to early 1900's. These were mounted on the outside of the car and hand pumped by the driver.

PLATE 154. Troubl Light, 8"l, convenien for providing ligh under hoods or vehicles

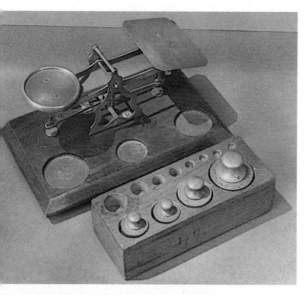

PLATE 155. Photographs 155 through 166 are examples of scales and weighing devices. Scales range from small ones used by post offices, pharmacies, and jewelers to larger types used by merchants for weighing candy, grain, meat and produce. This set is 8"l, 4"w, European.

PLATE 158. Round Scale with brass plate to calibrate pounds, marked "Chatillon."

PLATE 159. Scale, 23"l, iron ring and hook, marked "Landers Improved Spring Balance Warranted, 150 lbs.," American.

PLATE 156. Merchant's Scale, marked "J. Hart, Maker, Birmingham," English, mid 1800's.

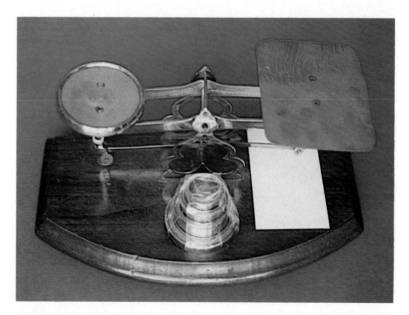

PLATE 157. Wooden and Brass Scales, 9"l, brass weights, European.

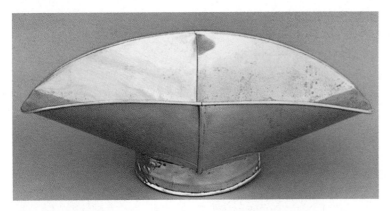

PLATE 160. Pan or "Scoops" used on spring or weight-type scales, American. This one has a pedestal base, 20"l.

PLATE 161. Balancing Scales, 11"l, French, mounted on walnut base.

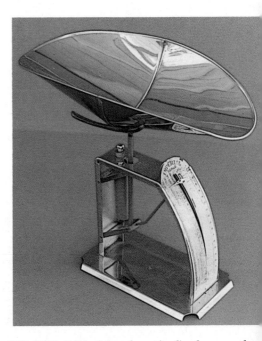

PLATE 163. Postage Scale, marking illegible.

PLATE 162. Scale, 13"l, English, marked "W. & T. Avery, Ltd., Birmingham."

PLATE 164. Merchant's Scale, marke "Imperial Scale, Gilfillan Scale & HDW Co Chicago," 9½"h.

PLATE 165. Measure for grain, 8½"h, 4 ½"d, marked "HOWE."

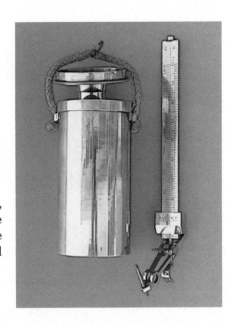

PLATE 166. Scale, 6½"h, measure, 9"l. The measure fits into the cylinder of the scale, rope handle, marked "Swedish Made."

PLATE 168. Cash Register, mounted on wooden base, similar but larger than the preceding one. Note the marble shelf and decoration.

PLATE 169. Telephone, candlestick style, 13"h, circa 1920's.

PLATE 167. Cash Register, 12"w. This one was made by the National Company, an American firm founded around the mid 1880's. Most examples of cash registers found on the market today were made by National. Various sizes, often ornately decorated, are seen.

PLATE 170. Telephone, similar style as the one preceding, except this one has a brass handle.

PLATE 172. Miniature Microscope, 3"h.

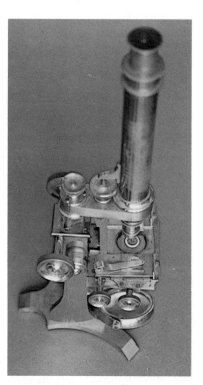

PLATE 171. Microscope, 17"h, inscribed "BAKER, 224 High Holborn, London," circa 1840.

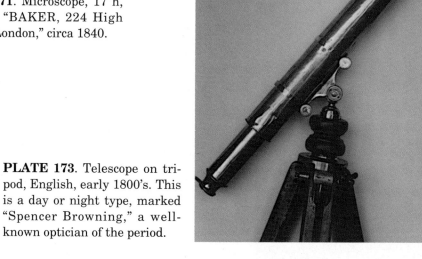

PLATE 173. Telescope on tripod, English, early 1800's. This is a day or night type, marked "Spencer Browning," a well-known optician of the period.

PLATE 174. American Survey Instrument, 17"l, inscribed "HERM PFISTER, Cincinnati."

PLATE 175. Tool Holder made of brass.

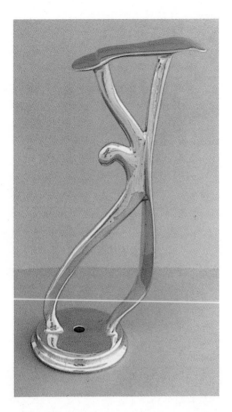

PLATE 178. One part of a Shoe-shine stand, 15"h.

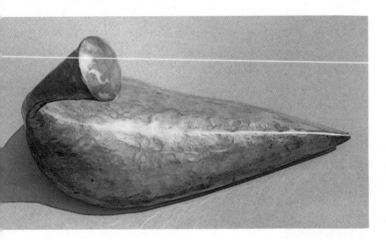

PLATE 176. Cobbler's Tool, red brass Shoe Mold, 11"x9".

PLATE 177. Chisel, red brass, 7½"l, marked "Beryl Co., S. 108," and "BE Co."

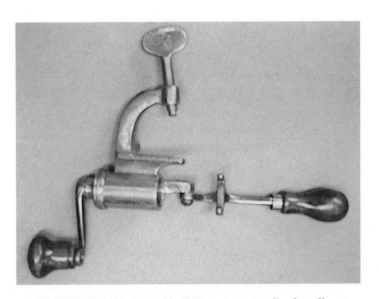

PLATE 179. Shotgun Shell Crimper, wooden handles.

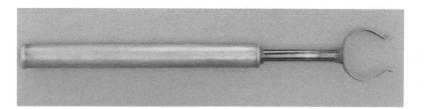

PLATE 180. Test Tube Holder, 8"l.

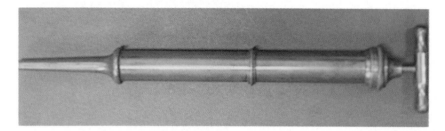

PLATE 181. Pump, 16½"l.

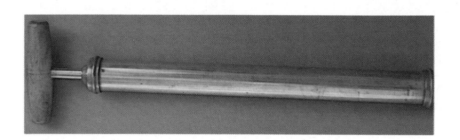

PLATE 182. Pump style Mister, marked "Whitney, Boston, Mass."

PLATE 184. Blow Torch, 7"h.

PLATE 183. Fishing Reels, circa mid to late 1800's.

PLATE 185. Cricket Box, 7"l, 5"w, wooden handle, note wire "cage" inside lid, marked "Brevette, S. G. D. G.," French, circa late 1800's.

PLATE 186. Blow Torch 11"l, marked "The Turner Brass Works, Sycamore, Ill." Trademark is a figure of a lady on a gym bar.

PLATE 188. Strainer, two parts, 3¾"h, 12"d, ring is formed from sheet brass joined by clamping and soldering, screen is also brass, marked "The Denver Fire Clay Company," circa late 1800's. This type of strainer was used at potteries or brick factories.

PLATE 187. Prickly Pear Burner, 22"h, marked "B. & H. Pear Burner Co., Sole Owner, Pearsall, TX, Pat. U. S. & Mexico.," circa early 1900's. These were used to burn the stickers off the prickly pears so that cattle could eat the pears.

PLATE 189. French Carbide Lantern with copper cover, 11½"h, marked "C. Quvrard & Cie."

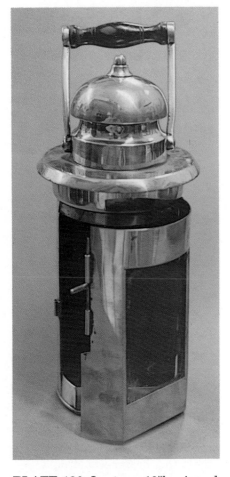

PLATE 190. Lantern, 10"h, pierced at top and bottom to allow air to enter, wooden handle.

PLATE 191. Pair of Lanterns, not a matched pair: left, 10½"h, base 3½"d, wooden handle, copper latch on door opening, perforated bottom; right, 10⅜"h, base, 3¼"d, wooden handle, perforated bottom, note difference in "bell" shape of the tops of the two lanterns, circa early 1900's.

PLATE 193. Lantern, marked "Dietz, New York, U.S.A., 1900, 13" h.

PLATE 194. A railroad collectible in the form of an Ash Tray for a passenger train, 5"l, attaches to seat, marked "N.F.R." and "L.N.E.R."

PLATE 192. Bracket Candleholder used on railroad cars and mounted to the wall. Originally this holder would have had a glass chimney. It is 8"h. Such holders are often used as sconces today.

PLATE 195. Keys to Railroad locks, from left to right: marked: "NEV CRR"; "CPRR of CAL"; "ETH & CRR, W. Bohannon, Brooklyn, New York."

PLATE 197. Coal Miner's Head Lamp, 4½"h, marked "Made in USA, Pat. Pending," by "JUST-RITE," and "United States of America" on base.

PLATE 196. Pair of Locks, 3"l, marked "W. Bohannon, Pat. June 25, 1878."

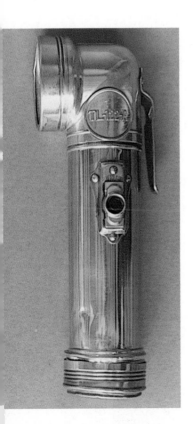

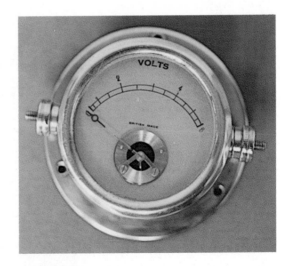

PLATE 200. Voltage meter, marked "British Made," 1¾"x 3½".

PLATE 198. Flash Light, nickel and brass, 7"l, marked "TL-122-A," circa 1930.

PLATE 199. Thermometer, 13"l, marked "Weksler, New York City."

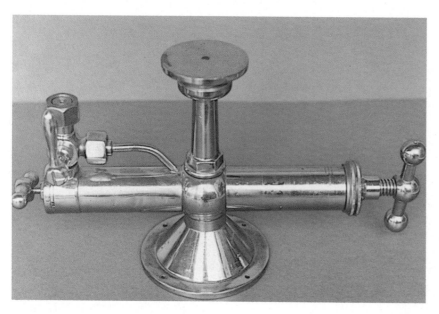

PLATE 201. Pressure Gauge Tester, marked "Schaffer & Budenberg Corp, Brooklyn, N.Y." 13½"l, 8¼"h.

PLATE 204. Hose Nozzle from a fire truck, shown alone and made into a lamp. The nozzle is marked "Elkhart Brass Mfg. Co., Indiana."

PLATE 202. Steam Whistle, 9¾"l, marked "Kinsley Mfg. Co., Bridgeport Co., USA."

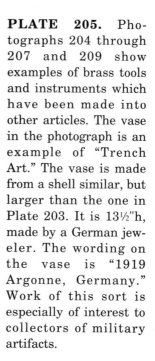

PLATE 205. Photographs 204 through 207 and 209 show examples of brass tools and instruments which have been made into other articles. The vase in the photograph is an example of "Trench Art." The vase is made from a shell similar, but larger than the one in Plate 203. It is 13½"h, made by a German jeweler. The wording on the vase is "1919 Argonne, Germany." Work of this sort is especially of interest to collectors of military artifacts.

PLATE 203. Brass Shell, 6½"l, 2"d, circa 1915.

PLATE 208. Plates 208 through 233 illustrate "Nautical" antiques and collectibles. Many of these date from the World War II period. Ship's Bell, 9"h.

PLATE 206. Fire Extinguisher made into a floor lamp.

PLATE 207. Brass Shell, 2 feet long, 105 millimeter, made into a table lamp.

PLATE 209. Table made from a brass Port Hole from a World War II Merchant Ship.

PLATE 210. Bilge Pump, 30"l, marked "S. H. Brooks, W. Randolph, VT, Patented Aug. 1884."

PLATE 212. Yacht Wheel, brass and mahogany, 28"d.

PLATE 211. A Buoy Safety Light is shown here.

PLATE 213. Propeller.

PLATE 214. Ship Reflector, English, marked "Kelvin & Hughes, Ltd., NKII REFLECTOR BINNACLE," 16"h, circa 1945.

PLATE 215. Fog Horn, 24"h, marked "Original Makrofon."

PLATE 217.
Dry Compass, 11½" x 6½", Marked "Kelvin & James White, Ltd., 13 Cambridge St., Glasgow."

PLATE 218. Brass Signal Cannon (in new carrier), 16"l, marked "1880, Big Boom."

PLATE 216. Life Boat Compass, 12" x 8½", marked "BERGEN-NAUTIK."

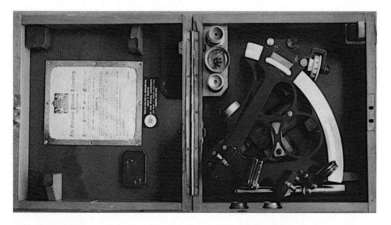

PLATE 219. Sextant, Scottish, with original label in top of case, World War II period.

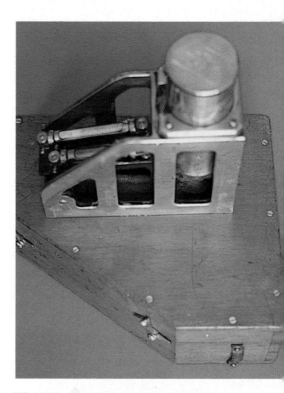

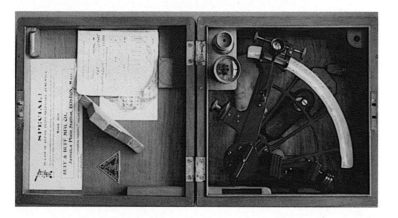

PLATE 220. Sextant, U.S. Navy, World War II.

PLATE 221. Clinometer, brass in mahogany case, 8" x 6", marked "45 Degrees, Admiralty Pattern, E.R. Watts & Son, London, No. 24288" World War II period.

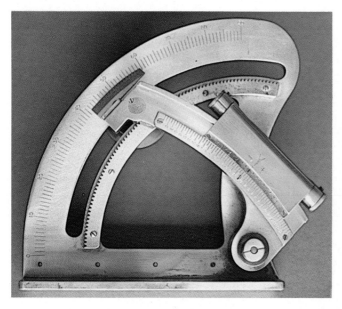

PLATE 222. Clinometer, 6¼"l, World War II period.

PLATE 223. Magnifier, 4"h, 9"d.

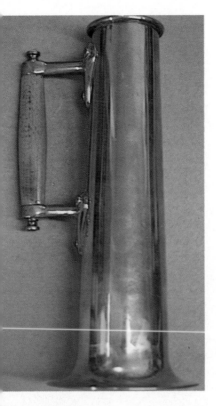

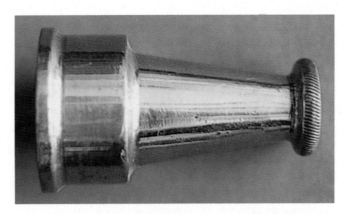

PLATE 227. Nozzle (fits on end of hoses), 3" h.

PLATE 224. Hydrometer, English, 2"h, made into a tankard.

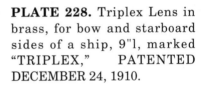

PLATE 228. Triplex Lens in brass, for bow and starboard sides of a ship, 9"l, marked "TRIPLEX," PATENTED DECEMBER 24, 1910.

PLATE 225. Yacht Tie-Down, 5"l.

PLATE 229. Bulkhead Light, marked "Lovell, Arlington, New Jersey, Oceanic." These lights are used in engine rooms and are explosion proof.

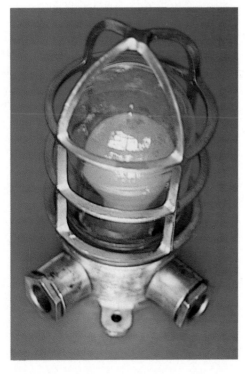

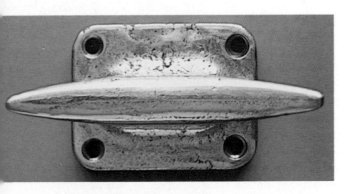

PLATE 226. Yacht Tie-Down, 6½"l.

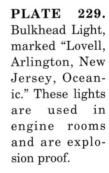

PLATE 230. Mast Head Lamp, 10"h, made by "A. Ward Hendrickson & Co., Inc., Brooklyn, New York," Note that the glass is supposed to be white but has turned purple from age and lead content.

PLATE 231. Brass Lantern with green glass indicating starboard or left light, marked "PERKO, Brooklyn." This lantern was made prior to World War II as the Perko Company moved to Florida during the war years.

PLATE 232. Anchor Lantern, 12"h.

PLATE 233. Ship's Kerosene Lamp, 4½"h (base), 12"h overall, note base is pierced for attachment to a flat surface.

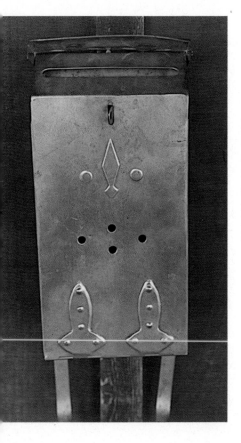

PLATE 234. The Hardware items featured in this section were made prior to the mid 20th century, although some of the styles are currently being copied today. Mail Box, 13"l with slot and key hole.

PLATE 236. Door Stop, 11⅜"h, base 4⅝"d, urn shape topped by a "swag" finger ring, cast brass with an iron insert for added weight; marked "Peerage" and "England" with interior stamped with "11486," circa late 1800's.

PLATE 235. Mail Box, envelope style with lion's head opener, circa mid 20th century.

PLATE 237. Door Bell, 7"d, with cast iron back, marked with patent dates of 1872, 1873, 1874.

PLATE 238. Door Knocker, 6"l, an ever popular style of lion's head with ring through nose.

PLATE 239. Commercial Door Handle, 14½"l.

PLATE 240. Name Plates for doors, 6"l.

PLATE 241. Door Knockers, 6½"l, in Art Deco style.

PLATE 242. Door Handles; Left wood and brass, 10½"l; Right ornately patterned handle, 11"l.

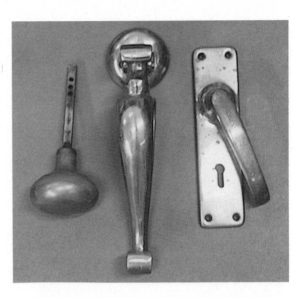

PLATE 244. Three early 20th century Door Handles: Left, Door Knob; Center, Door Handle and Knocker; Right, Door Handle with key hole opening.

PLATE 243. A selection of Door Knobs.

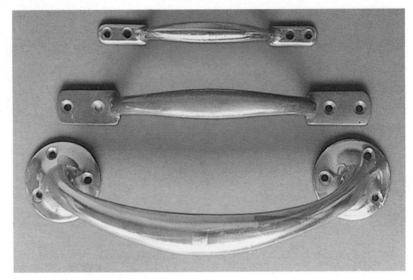

PLATE 245. Pulls for cabinets or chests.

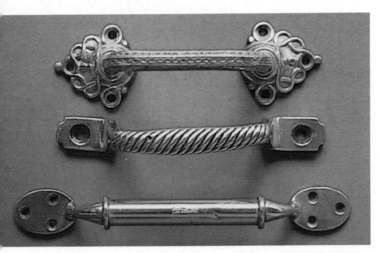

PLATE 246. Pulls for cabinets or chests. Price depends on size and ornateness of design.

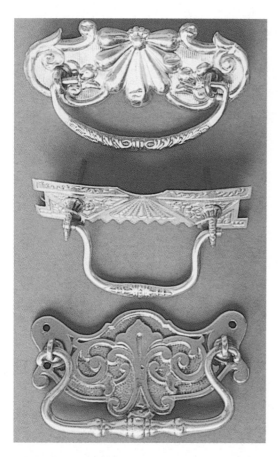

PLATE 248. Pulls for cabinets or chests with backplates and key hole openings.

PLATE 247. Pulls for cabinets or chests with backplates.

PLATE 249. Red brass Pulls for cabinets or chests.

PLATE 251. Ormolu, French: figural design on left, 11"l; floral and fruit garland design on right, 10"l.

PLATE 250. Ormolu (Furniture mounts), French, figural designs: Top, 3½"l; Bottom, 7½"l.

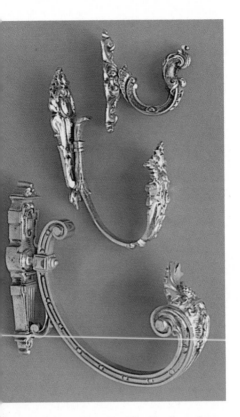

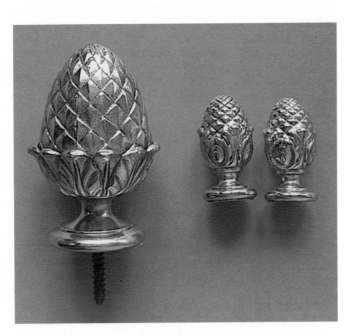

PLATE 255. Curtain Tie-Backs, pineapple design.

PLATE 252. Curtain Tie-Backs, showing one each of a pair.

PLATE 253. Curtain Tie-Backs: Left, knob style; Center, Art Deco design; Right, beaded decor on base.

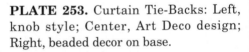
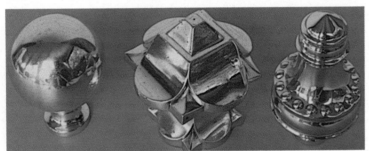

PLATE 254. Curtain Tie-Backs in three different designs.

PLATE 256. Brass Shower Ring and Head.

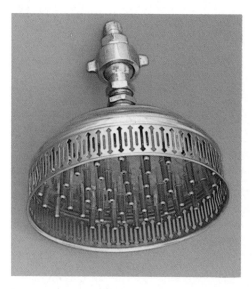

PLATE 257. Shower Head, 9½"d.

PLATE 258. Bathroom Cup Holder and Soap Dish, 8"l overall.

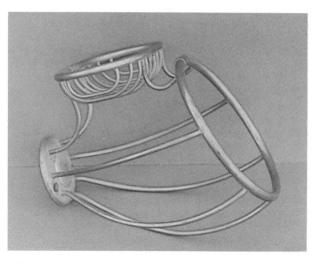

PLATE 259. Soap and Sponge Holder, 7½"l overall.

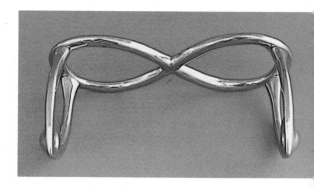

PLATE 260. Toilet Tissue Hanger, 6½"l, marke "SAN-O-LA."

PLATE 261. Towel Rack from railroad car, 33½"l.

PLATE 262. Sprinkler head for a garden hose, 4"l, circa early 1900's, American.

Decorative and Personal Objects

PLATE 263. Bowl and Pitcher set, Russian origin, mid to late 1800's. Pitcher sits on pierced insert.

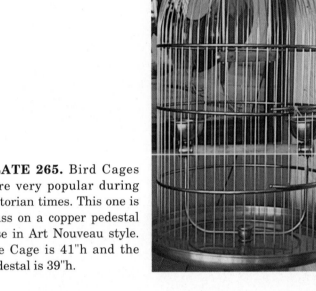

PLATE 265. Bird Cages were very popular during Victorian times. This one is brass on a copper pedestal base in Art Nouveau style. The Cage is 41"h and the Pedestal is 39"h.

PLATE 264. Bidet, (French of course!), on wrought iron stand, marked "MARQUE J.B., DEPOSE," 15½"h, 21"l, 19th century.

PLATE 266. Bird Cage, 39"h, 18½"d, circa mid 20th century.

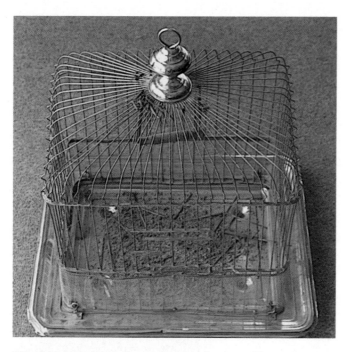

PLATE 267. Bird Cage, square shape, 16"h, with stand (not shown), circa mid 20th century.

PLATE 268. Bird Cage, 16"h, with stand (not shown), circa mid 20th century.

PLATE 269. Boxes made entirely of brass or decorated with brass have been made in a variety of styles and for a variety of purposes through the years. Several types are shown in photographs 269 to 275 and 277 to 278. This one is oval shaped, French, circa 1800, 8½"l, 3"w.

PLATE 270. Bride's Box, 13"sq., 9"h, from India, circa 1850.

PLATE 271. Brass and Jade Box, marked "China," 6"l.

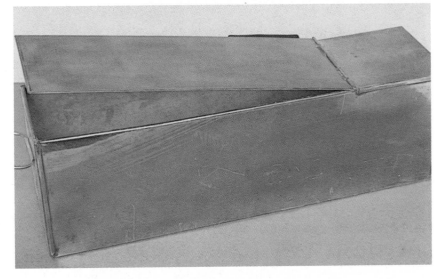

PLATE 272. Safety Deposit Box, 18½"l, 4½"w.

PLATE 274. Brass, Jade and Ivory Box, unmarked, 11"l.

PLATE 273. Box, 2"h, 4½"l, 3½"w, sheet brass over wood, griffin design accented with foliage, handmade in the Arts and Crafts style; marked "T&C Chicago" and "F. R. & Co. New York" in circle with "F. H. Deknatel Copyright 1910" in stamp form on felt covered base; interior fabric lined.

PLATE 276. Playing Card Case, 3½" x 2⅜", marked Smoleroff Kard Pack Pat Pend," monogrammed "E.J.C.," American, circa. 1920's.

PLATE 275. Brass Box, 3"h, 10½"w, wooden bottom, velvet lined, engraved figural scene on top.

PLATE 277. Candy Box, made for Schrafft's, transfer colonial design on top, 8"l, 5"w.

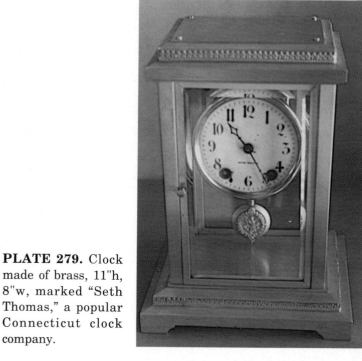

PLATE 279. Clock made of brass, 11"h, 8"w, marked "Seth Thomas," a popular Connecticut clock company.

PLATE 278. Brass and Enamel Box, 6½"l, 2½"w, Oriental.

PLATE 280. Clock, 10"h, 5½"w, porcelain face, marked "Made in France."

PLATE 281. A number of desk related items are shown in Plates 281 to 296. Book Ends, 3¾"h, 4½"w, cast golfing figures in an Art Deco style, marked "Art Brass Co. N.Y.," circa 1920's.

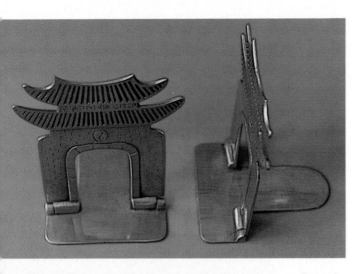

PLATE 282. Pair of brass Book Ends made in a Pagoda style, 6"h, 4"w, marked "China."

PLATE 283. Book Ends, 6"h, 5½"l, Unicorn and Lion design, English, mid 20th century.

PLATE 284. Brass Desk Accessory with Letter Holder, 7"h, 12"l, 10"d, European.

PLATE 285. Brass Crest 12"x11", figural design of Lions and Unicorn, French, inscribed *"Honi Soit Qui Mal Y Pense,"* an old French saying "Evil be to him who evil thinks." These are sometimes used as "Door Porters" (door stops).

PLATE 286. Desk Set: Inkwell, Letter Holder, and Blotter, simple shape and design reflecting the Art Deco period, American, circa 1920's.

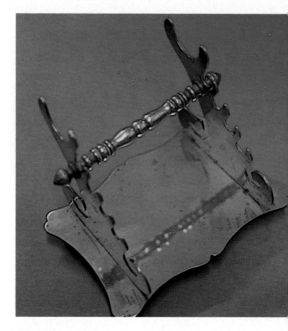

PLATE 289. Pen Staff Holder, 6" x 6¼", European.

PLATE 287. Letter Holder, 3½"h, 5"w, marked "Bradley & Hubbard," American, circa 1920's.

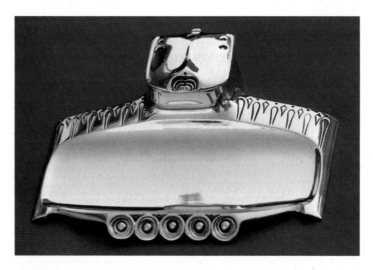

PLATE 288. Inkstand, 7½"l, 6¼"w, cast brass with molded design in an Art Nouveau style, European, circa early 1900's.

PLATE 290. Brass and copper Desk Accessory with pen tip drawer, inkwell and pen holders, footed, pierced at top for hanging, English, 8"h, 8"l.

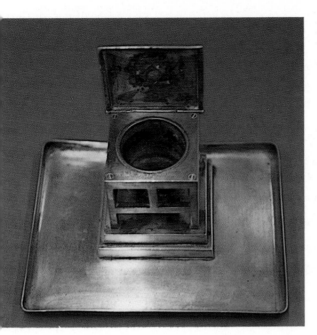

PLATE 291. Inkwell with tray, 3½"h, tray 6"l, circa mid 20th century.

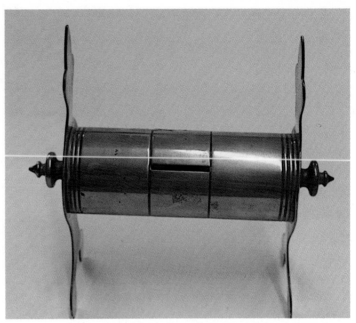

PLATE 294. Bank, English, Victorian.

PLATE 292. Inkwell Set, 8"l, 4½"w, English.

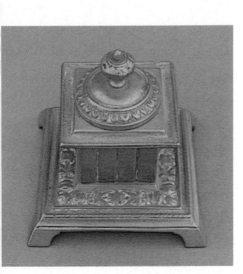

PLATE 293. Inkwell, 5"h, signed "Stingl."

PLATE 295. Water Carafe, 8"h, marked "Maxwell Phillips, New York," circa mid 20th century.

PLATE 296.
Letter Opener, 10¼"l, pierced work on blade, gargoyle design on handle.

PLATE 297. English thoroughbred and jockey Cast Figure, 7"l, 3¾"h equipped with feet at back to enable piece to stand upright, English, circa mid to late 1800's.

PLATE 298. Horse Brasses are interesting collector items which are found in quite a variety of designs as illustrated in this and the following two pictures.

PLATE 299. Horse Brasses mounted for display.

PLATE 300. Horse Brasses (for the ear).

PLATE 301. Censer or Incense Burner with chain, a type used in churches, intricate open-work construction, Oriental.

PLATE 302. Incense Burner, elephant motif in relief, bamboo style handles, Oriental.

PLATE 305. Planter or Jardiniere, pedestal base, lion head handles, English circa mid to late 18th century.

PLATE 303. Jardiniere, thick ball-shaped feet, lion's head handles, 6½"h, 9½"d, English.

PLATE 306. Jardiniere, reserves decorated with engraved bird and tree designs.

PLATE 304. Brass Bucket, 11"h, 10½"w, footed, applied animal designs, English, circa early 1800's.

PLATE 307. Jardiniere, 12"h, 17"d, lion head handles, English, early 18th century.

PLATE 308. Jardiniere, 4"h, 4"d, English, circa mid 20th century.

PLATE 310. Planter, 4½"h, Egyptian motif on front and back in an Art Deco style, European, circa 1920's.

PLATE 309. Jardiniere, miniature size, 2½"h, 3"d, marked "Chase." (Chase was a brass and copper company located in Waterbury, Connecticut), circa mid 20th century.

PLATE 311. Planter, 3½", 7"d, stamped design, fitted with a tin liner (r) which has a brass collar, English, circa late 1800's.

PLATE 312. Jardiniere, 6"h, 8"d (base replaced), oval medallions with embossed scroll designs.

PLATE 313. Brass and Copper Wall Vase, 6½"l, English.

PLATE 315. Vase, 8½"h, conical shape, very heavy, Oriental, circa mid 20th century.

PLATE 316. Jardiniere, footed, embossed grapes, English, 8"h, 7¼"d, circa mid 20th century.

PLATE 314. Brass Wall Ornament. This is often referred to as a Comb Holder, but Schiffer (p. 22, 1978) notes that is not really the function of this piece and in fact, its use has not been actually determined. It dates from the early 19th century.

PLATE 317. Wall Pocket Vase made in form of a bed warmer, embossed fruit designs, marked "Made in England," circa mid 20th century.

PLATE 319. Carriage Vases, 10"l.

PLATE 318. Vases, leaf and branch decor in relief, 10½"h, French, Art Nouveau period.

PLATE 320. Bras Vase Holder (woul have glass insert) 13½"h, intricate cut-ou work, circa mid 20t century.

PLATE 321. Pair of Vases, 13"h, figural and floral designs in relief, twisted serpent form handles, circa mid 20th century.

PLATE 323. Mirror, easel type, cast brass in an ornate Victorian design, marked "V M" with initials separated by the design of an iron betty lamp, circa late 1800's.

PLATE 322. Pair of Vases, 9½"h, embossed roses around center, originally silver plated, circa mid 20th century.

PLATE 324. Shaving Mirror in brass case, 21"h, 21"w, circa mid to late 1800's.

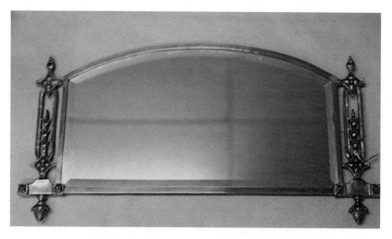

PLATE 325. Mirror, 15" x 30", in brass frame

PLATE 326. Brass Frame, 6"x8", circa mi 20th century.

PLATE 327. Hand Mirrors with brass frames and handles. The round mirror on the left and the oval one on the right have the same figural nude design on the handle in an Art Nouveau style.

PLATE 329. Perfume Vial incased in elaborately designed brass holder.

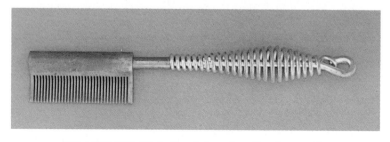

PLATE 328. Hair Straightening Comb, 10½"l.

98

PLATE 330. Group of Thimbles

PLATE 333. Cuspidor or Spittoon, 11¾"h, American, circa early 1900's.

PLATE 331. Opera Glasses, 3"l, 2½"w, French, marked "Lepine, Paris."

PLATE 334. Spittoon, hammered border, 5"h, 7"w.

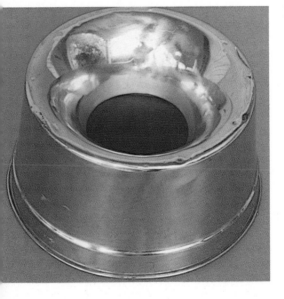

PLATE 332. Smoking and Tobacco accessories are shown in Photographs 332 through 348. Spittoon Cover, 5"h, 7"w.

PLATE 335. Spittoon, 3¼"h, 7¼"d, made in two pieces, marked "Farris Mfg. Co., Decatur, Illinois."

PLATE 336. Tobacco Jar, 8"h, circa mid 20th century.

PLATE 338. Cigar Holder combined with an Ash Tray, Match Holder, and Cigar Cutter, mounted on a wooden base, circa first quarter 20th century, American.

PLATE 337. Match Holder, 4½"h, circa mid 20th century.

PLATE 339. Ash Tray, circa mid 20th century.

PLATE 342. Ash tray, 1"h, 1⅔ d", individual hand-held type, cast construction, American, circa 1920's.

PLATE 340. Ash Trays with tortoise shell trim, 3½"d. The trim increases the price of this pair.

PLATE 341. Ash Tray, 5½"sq., hand hammered with repoussé design in the Arts & Crafts manner, American, circa first quarter 20th century.

PLATE 343. Advertising Ash Tray, "Smoke Fresh CRAVEN A," printed on leather, 4"h, 3½"d, circa mid 20th century.

PLATE 348. Tobacco Jar, 8"h, cast Colonial figure sitting on a barrel decorates top and serves as handle, three knob feet, English, mid to late 1800's.

PLATE 344. Brass Match Holder in barrel shape, 2½"h.

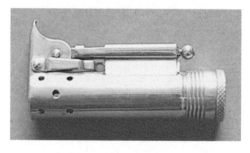

PLATE 345. Lighter, 2½"h, marked "Made in Austria."

PLATE 346. Match Holder with attached tray, 4"h.

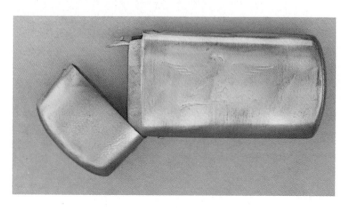

PLATE 347. Match Safe, Eagle design engraved on front.

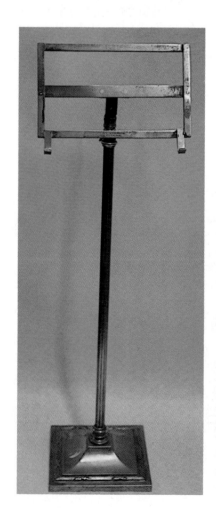

PLATE 349. Reading Stand, adjustable, marked "S. & S. Sheldon, Birmingham," English.

PLATE 350. Pedestal or Stand, 39"h, 14"d, French, early to mid 1800's.

PLATE 351. Table, 25½", 23½"d, factory made in the Arts and Crafts manner (original label missing); the top is hammered tin with a zinc coating and banded in brass; supported by a quarter sawn oak post mounted on a wooden base covered with machine hammered sheet brass, circa first quarter 20th century.

PLATE 352. Stool, 3 legs, 14"h, 12"d, English, chased designs on seat.

PLATE 353. Wall Plaques, 6½"d, English, circa mid 20th century. "Anne Hathaways Cottage" and "Robert Burns" are embossed on these souvenir plaques.

PLATE 354. Toy related item, Doll Bed, 23½"l, 13"h.

PLATE 356. Umbrella Stand embossed design of woman and two children, Dutch.

PLATE 355. White Brass Portrait Plaque, 9¼"d.

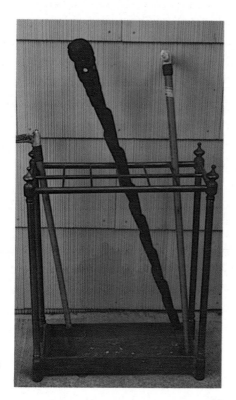

PLATE 357. Umbrella or Cane Stand, 19½"h, 25"w, French.

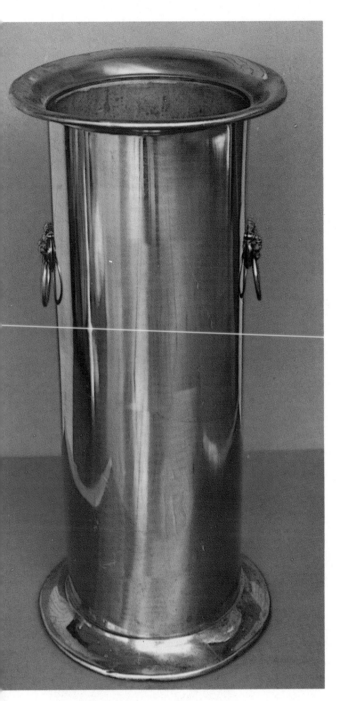

PLATE 358. Umbrella Stand with lion head handles, red brass, circa mid 20th century.

PLATE 359. Umbrella Stand, 19"h, base, 8¼"d, sheet brass with machine stamped design, marked "Made in England" with registry number, circa first quarter of the 20th century.

105

Antique Copper

Household Copper–Entrance & Foyer

PLATE 361. Outdoor Lighting Fixture, Sconce, 12"l, brass trim, hammered body.

PLATE 360. Outdoor Lighting Fixture, Porch Lantern, 22"h, cage-style construction, Victorian.

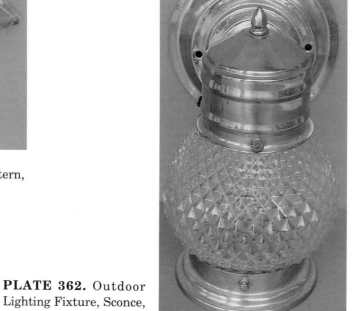

PLATE 362. Outdoor Lighting Fixture, Sconce, 9"l, pressed glass globe, lacquered.

PLATE 365. Outdoor Lighting Fixture, Gas Porch Lantern, 24"h, English.

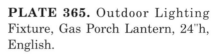

PLATE 363. Outdoor Lighting Fixture, Porch Light, 14"h, copper and brass, marked "Brooklyn, New York."

PLATE 364. Outdoor Lighting Fixture, Hanging Lantern, 9½"h, celluloid shade, pierced work on top, probably Oriental.

PLATE 366. Mirror, 31"l, 25¼"w, Copper Frame, 6"d, ornate embossed designs, Victorian.

PLATE 367. Jardiniere, 28"h overall. Planter is 25¼"d, repoussé decor, Victorian.

PLATE 368. Umbrella Stand, 19½"h, lacquered, made from an early 20th century American fire extinguisher.

PLATE 370. Planter, 15¼"h, 13¼"d, brass lion heads decor, brass paw feet, English, 19th century.

PLATE 369. Jardiniere, applied brass decoration on planter, ornately shaped three-legged brass stand, English, Victorian.

108

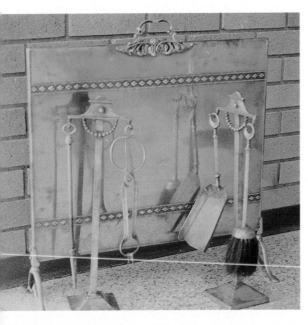

PLATE 371. Fire Back, 21"h, 22"w; Fireplace Tools for coal fires, English.

PLATE 372. Coal Scuttle, 16"h, pedestal base, tin lined, lacquered.

PLATE 373. Fire Back, 29"h, 27"w; Fender, 53½"l; and Tinder Boxes made into seats, scenic decor in high relief featuring a dog and her pups, Scottish.

PLATE 374. Coal Scuttle, 18"h, hammered body, embossed floral designs on top, Victorian.

PLATE 376. Coal Box, 18"h, brass medallions mounted on sides, brass paw feet.

PLATE 375. Coal Scuttle, 16"l, lacquered finish, note the slight differences in design between this one and the scuttle in photograph 372.

PLATE 377. Coal Box, 17"h, (liner not shown), shell and ring handles, marked "British Made."

PLATE 379. Coal or Peat Bucket, 10"h, 9"d, dovetailed construction, possibly Dutch.

PLATE 378. Coal Box on wrought iron stand. Box is 22"h, 26"w, 11½"d, lacquered, designed in Art Nouveau style, English.

PLATE 380. Log Container, 27"h, 22"w, hammered surface, brass paw feet, Georgian, early 1800's.

PLATE 382. Coal Bucket, 18"h, including wrought iron handle, hand hammered body.

PLATE 381. Coal Box, 16"h, 16"l, footed, urn finial, brass fittings, English.

111

PLATE 383. Silent Butler style Ash Container, 7½"w, 11"l. The size of this piece indicates that it was meant for collecting ashes from the hearth rather than from ash trays.

PLATE 384. Stove Insert, 26"h, 20"w, repoussé work in Art Nouveau style.

PLATE 385. Fire Back, 28"h, 17"w, sheet copper decorated with embossed peacock design, mounted on wrought iron frame in an Art Nouveau design.

PLATE 386. Table Lamp, electric marked "1928, Armour Bronze Core," lacquered, Art Deco lines.

PLATE 388. Planter, 4"h, 5½"d, marked "China."

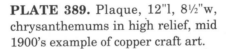

PLATE 38.. ..que, 14"d, fluted border, embossed roses.

PLATE 389. Plaque, 12"l, 8½"w, chrysanthemums in high relief, mid 1900's example of copper craft art.

PLATE 390. Coffee Table, faux bamboo handles and legs, Arts and Crafts period.

PLATE 391. Planter, 9"h, 10"d, copper body, brass handles and paw feet.

PLATE 394. Pair of copper and brass vases, 12"h, red jewels, Grecian design, mounted in allegorical figural bases, Victorian.

PLATE 392. Wall Pocket Planter, 5¾"h, 6"w, simple design indicates this piece was made during the 1920's.

PLATE 395. Pair of Vases, 13"h, embossed Egyptian motif, Art Deco period.

PLATE 393. Miniature Planters, 2"h, 4"w, made from a sheet of thick copper, circa early 1900's.

PLATE 396. Candleholder, 7¾"h, hand hammered work in an abstract tulip design from the Arts and Crafts movement, marked with a tree and name (illegible), probably English origin.

PLATE 398. Plaque, 26"l, 22"w, repoussé figural and floral decor of Art Nouveau era, English.

PLATE 397. Plaque, 10½" x 9", oval shape, dancing gypsy woman with tambourines and baby faun depicted in high relief in an allegorical design, marked "Tinant" at base.

PLATE 399. Desk Set: Blotter Holder, Inkwell, Pen Tray, hammered surfaces.

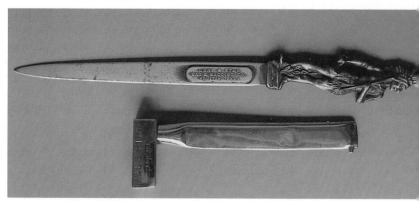

PLATE 401. Advertising Souvenirs: Hammer, 8"l, marked "Hale Fir[e] Pumps," and Letter Opener, 12"l, marked "Lone Star Bag and Baggin[g] Co., Houston, Texas."

PLATE 400. Wall Pocket Letter Holder, 9"h.

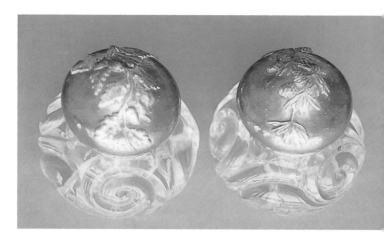

PLATE 403. Pair of Master Inkwells, 4½"h, heavy crystal bases tops decorated with embossed fruit and leaves, Victorian.

PLATE 402. Inkwell, hammered copper and cast brass, Art Deco design.

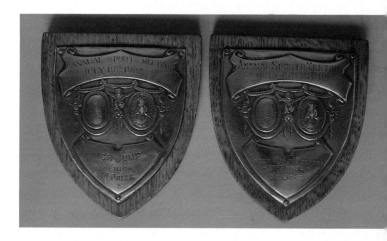

PLATE 404. Pair of Copper Award Plaques: Left, inscribe[d] "July 19th, 1922, High Jump Senior, 1st Prize"; Right, "Annua[l] Sports Meeting, High Jump Junior, July 21, 1920."

PLATE 405. Loving Cup, 13"h, two handles.

PLATE 406. Souvenir Bank from The Plains National Bank, Lubbock, Texas.

PLATE 407. Box, 10½"h, 8½"w, 2½"h, wooden, decorated with a sheet of copper which was hand hammered to portray a Victorian woman cutting flowers in her garden.

PLATE 408. Covered Jar, 5"h, 4"d, ring design with a brass base and lid and a copper body, tinned interior; probably a candy jar, Art Deco style, circa 1920's.

117

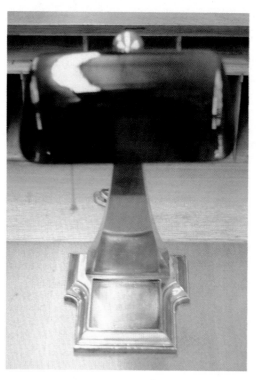

PLATE 409. Desk Lamp, cast copper with dark green glass shade, marked "Amronlite Made in U. S. A., Patent May 20th, 1917."

PLATE 411. Bird Cage, 14"h, copper and brass marked "Made in U. S. A., Hendryx, New Haven Conn."

PLATE 410. Smoking Set: Match Holder, Cigarette Container, Ash Tray, displayed on a 10" Tray, hammered and cut-out work from the Arts and Crafts era.

PLATE 412. Cowboy Hat Ash Tray, commemorative of the 1926 Dallas Cotton Palace.

PLATE 413. Match Holder in form of a cowboy boot, 4"h.

PLATE 415. Gun Powder Flask, 7½"l, embossed dead game, brass fittings.

PLATE 414. Snuff Case, 3½"l, 3"w, copper, brass, and silver; shovel, 2"l.

119

PLATE 417. Coffee Pot, 10"h, engraved and repoussé work, lacquered.

PLATE 416. Coffee Pot, 9"h, wooden handle and finial, hinged spout cover, embossed fleur-de-lis on spout, French or Canadian origin, lacquered.

PLATE 419. Coffee Pot, 12"h, goose-neck spout, brass finial, extended wooden handle, circa mid-1800's, English.

PLATE 418. Coffee Pot, 11½"h, wooden handle, hinged brass spout cover, "Majestic" (brand) embossed on lid, lacquered.

PLATE 420. Coffee Pot, 10"h, wooden handle, brass finial, hinged spout cover, marked "Rome Metalware" on base, battered and mended.

PLATE 422. Coffee Pot, 10"h, brass lid, engraved body design, originally plated.

PLATE 423. Percolator, urn style, electric, marked "Manning Quality Bowman, Meriden, Conn., patented 1910," lacquered, originally silver plated; covered Sugar and Creamer.

PLATE 421. Percolator, 7"h, small four-cup size.

PLATE 424. Percolator, urn style, brass stand with burner, 14"h overall, marked "Patented March 20, 1906, and July 17, 1906," lacquered.

PLATE 427. Coffee Pot, 14"h, camp fire style, brass fittings, iron and wood handle, American.

PLATE 425. Percolator, urn style, copper and brass, electric, marked "Universal," lacquered.

PLATE 426. Percolator, 14"h, 10"w, copper and brass with Bakelite handles, marked "Keystone Wear," with two plates on inside marked "9-28" and "11-48," which seemingly indicate the dates of assembly.

PLATE 428. Coffee Pot, 13"h, wooden handle and finial, Art Deco shape.

PLATE 429. Biscuit Barrel, 5¾"h, 5⅜"d, hand hammered work from the Arts and Crafts era, marked with a hammer and anvil mark and "Hand Made Craftsman Co." with form number "878."

PLATE 430. Coal Carrier, 33½"l, iron and wooden handle, simple punched work on lid, English, 19th century.

PLATE 431. Coal Carrier, 39"l, fancy pierced lid, English, 19th century.

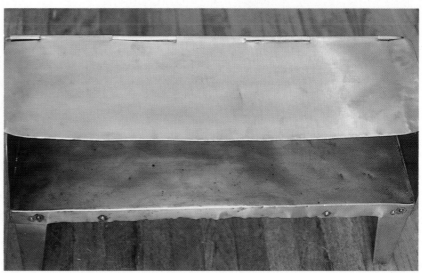

PLATE 432. Warming Oven, 11"h, 23½"l, hinged top, English.

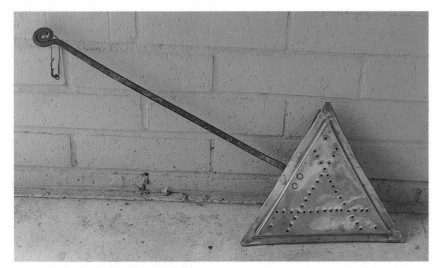

PLATE 433. Chestnut Roaster, 23"l, iron handle, hand-punched design on lid.

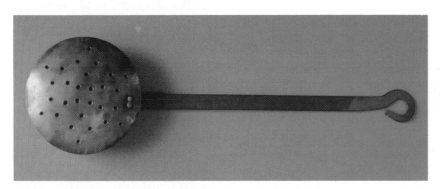

PLATE 434. Chestnut Roaster, iron handle, 16"l, pierced lid.

PLATE 435. Colander, 26"l, 12½"d, tin lined, pierced work forms design on base.

PLATE 436. Tinderbox Base, 3"h, 6"d.

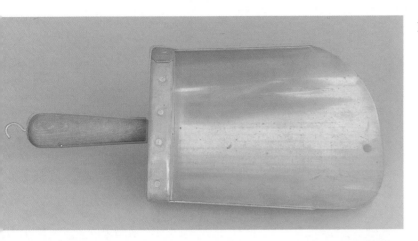

PLATE 437. Scoop, 14"l, 6"w, lacquered.

PLATE 438. Scoops made into candle sconces.

PLATE 439. Two part Strainer or Sieve, 6"h, 12½"d, marked "Caskell & Chambers Friar Filter."

PLATE 440. Tea Caddy, 6"h, simple engraved pattern on front, badly dented.

PLATE 441. Dipper, 7½"d, 26"l, brass handle.

PLATE 444. Candy Pan, 14"d, iron handles, lacquered.

PLATE 443. Skimmer, 7½"d, 34"l, iron handle.

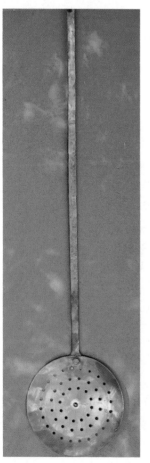

PLATE 442. Skimmer, 5"w, 22"l, pierced bowl, copper handle.

PLATE 445. Preserving Kettle, 25"d, iron handles, soldering visible around bottom half of pan.

126

PLATE 446. Apple Butter Kettle, 13"h, 21½"d, set in three-legged iron stand, with wooden stirrer, American, mid 1800's.

PLATE 447. Preserving Kettle, 26"d, iron andles.

127

PLATE 448. Preserving Kettle, iron bail handle, brass fittings, Argentina origin, circa mid 1800's.

PLATE 449. Preserving Kettle, 4"h, 8"d, iron handles, circa mid 1800's.

PLATE 450. Preserving Kettle, 8"h, 13"d, dovetailed on sides, simple soldering on base.

PLATE 451. Preserving Kettle, 18"h, 30"d, hammered body.

128

PLATE 452. Jelly Kettle or Pail, tin lined, 11"h, 12½"d.

PLATE 454. Stewing Kettle, 5½"h, 8"d.

PLATE 453. Preserving Kettle, 11"h, 23"d, cast iron reinforced rim.

PLATE 455. Stewing Kettle, 6"h, 9"d, Mid-East origin.

PLATE 456. Stewing Kettle, 8½"h, 13½"d, dovetailed construction.

PLATE 458. Stewing Kettle, 10"h, 12"d, narrow, notched dovetailed work near base.

PLATE 457. Stewing Kettle, 11"h, 14"d, soldered on base.

PLATE 459. Stewing Kettle, 9"h, 15½"d repaired base, American, 19th century.

PLATE 460. Stewing Kettle, 8½"h, 22"d, fancy
forged iron bail.

PLATE 461. Copper bucket, 14½"h, 12"d, a well
executed handmade and hand hammered piece
with iron bail and copper riveted iron bail ears
(note ears do not match). The piece was made in
three parts with brass brazed seams which are
hidden by the exterior strapping; European origin,
circa early to mid 1800's.

PLATE 463. Syrup
Jug with funnel
spout, American,
New England, 19th
century.

PLATE 462. Pail, 9½"h, 11"d, hammered surface, note simple brass soldered seam.

PLATE 464. Hot Liquid Measure, 7"h.

PLATE 465. Measure, 8"h, tin lined
marked "Kreamer."

PLATE 466. Set of Hot Liquid Measu
originally tinned, hammered surfaces, l
quered: left 5"h, center, 3½"h; right, 3"h.

PLATE 467. Measures in graduated sizes,
tin lined, lacquered. Sizes: 10"h, 5½"h, 4½"h,
3¼"h, 2¾"h, 2"h. The measures are similar
but not a matched set; one (5½"h) marked
"Nosco."

PLATE 470. Measure, 2½"h, marked "½", (cup); Measure, 2"h, marked "⅓" (cup).

PLATE 468. Double Measure, 8¼"l, pint (bottom) and half-pint (top) capacity.

PLATE 469. Measure, 5½"h, tin lined, brass trim.

PLATE 471. Mold, 9"h, marked "Dartnall," English, 19th century.

133

PLATE 475. Mold, cross form, 6"h, English, 19th century.

PLATE 472. Mold, 7½"h, rose and leaf design, English.

PLATE 476. Mold, 5"h, 6"d, English, 19th century.

PLATE 473. Mold, 4"h, 5"d, "P.S." engraved on base, English, 19th century.

PLATE 474. Mold, 4"h, 4"d, marked "J.L. & Co.," English, 19th century.

PLATE 477. Mold, 7¼"l, 5"d, oval shape, English, 19th century.

PLATE 478. Tube Mold, 4"h, 8"d, German, late 19th century.

PLATE 481. Ring Mold, 6"d, English, 19th century.

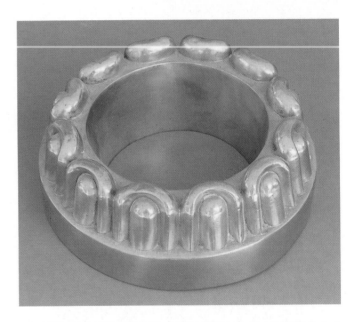

PLATE 482. Ring Mold, 2½"h, 7"d, marked "273," Art Deco design, English.

PLATE 479. Mold with crockery insert and wire bail handle, early 20th century.

PLATE 483. Oval Mold, tin base and collar, grape pattern, English, 19th century.

PLATE 480. Tube Mold, 2½"h, 5½"d, 20th century.

135

PLATE 484. Mold, tin base (collar missing), crown pattern, English, 19th century.

PLATE 485. Mold, 10"l, fruit basket design, 20th century.

PLATE 486. Tube Mold, 5"h, six-sided, floral pattern on top, English, 19th century.

PLATE 487. Tube Mold, 5"h, round base with top shaped into six sides, English, 19th century.

PLATE 488. Tube Mold, 10½"d, German, early 20th century.

PLATE 491. Tube Mold, 4"h, 7"d, 20th century.

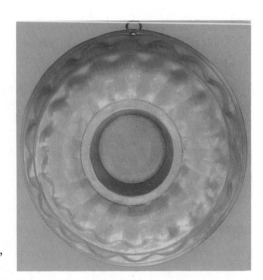

PLATE 492. Tube Mold, 11"d, early 20th century.

PLATE 489. Mold, 3"h, 4¼"d, German, hammered surface, early 20th century.

PLATE 490. Mold 11½"d, simple design, early 20th century.

PLATE 493. Mold, 5¼"h, 9"d, cross design, wire bail handle. German, early 20th century.

PLATE 494. Milk Pitcher, 7½"h, 6½"d, hinged lid, Russian, 19th century.

PLATE 497. Water Can, 9"h, tin top circa mid 1800's.

PLATE 495. Pitcher, 8½"h, Art Nouveau style, English.

PLATE 496. Syrup Pitcher, 6"h, dovetailed construction, 19th century.

PLATE 498. Water Can, 12"h, 10"d, tinned interior iron handles, brass spigot and fittings.

138

PLATE 499. Watering Pail, 11½"h, base, 6½"d, clean-cut lines featuring a combination of hand and factory work, circa early 1900's.

PLATE 501. Pitcher, 15"h, engraved design of Lion and Unicorn with old French saying "Honi Soit Qui Mal Y Pense" (evil be to him who thinks evil), marked "England" and "Celebrate."

PLATE 500. Pitcher, 9"h, tin lined, circa mid 1800's.

PLATE 502. Pitcher or Jug, 7"h, hammered body, tin lined.

PLATE 503. Set of Colonial Mexican Pitchers, 8", 7", 6" in height, hammered bodies, dovetailed, tin lined.

PLATE 504. Pitcher, 8"h, hammered body, unlined, attractive curved handle attached only to the top of the piece.

PLATE 506. Stock Pot, 13"h, 10"d, brass handles, stamped "Clarendon, Hammersmith," English, 19th century.

PLATE 505. Stock Pot, 19½"h, tin lid.

PLATE 507. Stock Pot, 20"h, wooden handles, brass and copper spigot, lacquered.

PLATE 508. Stock Pot, 20½"h, 19"d, brass handles, spigot missing, English, 19th century.

PLATE 509. Steamer, 24"l, 15"w, 10"h, iron handle, English, 19th century.

PLATE 510. Vegetable Steamer, 8½", 14"d, brass handle, English.

PLATE 511. Steamer, 5"h, 15"l, with drainer (not shown).

PLATE 512. Fish Kettle (lid missing), 14"l, 9"d, tin lined, brass handles, English, mid 1800's.

PLATE 513. Clam Steamer, 11"h, 8"d, marked "Fried, Loblich, Wien," Austrian.

PLATE 514. Covered Sauce Pan, 10½"h, 10"d. Lid is marked "F.A.
Walker & Co., Cornhill, Boston, Mass," hammered surface, lion handles,
lacquered, circa early 20th century.

PLATE 515. Sauce Pan, 9"h, 6"d,
iron handle, lacquered, marked "P.
Palmier, Ortega 34, Mexico," 20th
century.

PLATE 516. Sauce Pan, 5¼"h, 9"d, dovetailed on base, iron handle, 19th century.

PLATE 517. Sauce Pan, 7"h, 6½"d, 19th century.

PLATE 518. Covered Sauce Pan, 11"h, 14"d, iron handles, dovetailed, 19th century.

PLATE 519. Sauce Pan, 5"h, 9½"d, brass handle.

PLATE 520. Sauce Pan, 3"h, 12"d, dovetailed, New England, 19th century.

PLATE 521. Set of Sauce Pans: 7¼"d, 5½"d, 5"d, 4½"d, 3½"d; brass handles, French, circa mid 20th century.

PLATE 522. Sauce Pan, 5"h, 8"d, dovetailed, iron handle, marked "C.C. Mutual, Catherine, N.Y."

PLATE 523. Skillet, 2½"h, 9½"d, dovetailed, hammered surface, iron handle, lacquered, 19th century.

PLATE 524. Skillet, 2"h, 10¼"d, hammered body, iron handle.

PLATE 525. Ebleskiver Pan, 3"h, 11"d.

PLATE 526. Ebleskiver Pan, 3"h, 11"d, ring hook.

PLATE 527. Escargot Pan, 2½"h, 18"d.

PLATE 528. Baking Pan, 5½"h, 8"d, tin lined, brass handles.

PLATE 529. Roasting Pan, 27"l, 20"w, 7"h, diamond shaped, English, 19th century.

PLATE 530. Baking Pan, 2½"h, 11½"d, ring hook.

PLATE 531. Two-Part Baking Pan or Cooker, "h, 8"d, tin lined. Top could serve as lid, separate pan, or plate.

PLATE 532. Baking Pan, 19¾"d, 3¾" deep, hammered body with handrolled rim over an iron rod, equipped with a steel hanging rod attached with copper rivets, originally tin lined, circa mid to late 1800's.

PLATE 533. Baking Pan, 2½"h, 11½"d, iron ring hook, hammered surface, originally tinned.

PLATE 534. Baking Pan, 13½"d, 2¾" deep, similar in construction to one in Plate 532, circa mid to late 1800's.

PLATE 535. Baking Pans, Left, 3"h, 4¼"d; Right, 3¼"h, 5¼"d. Left is marked "G. Fontana, London."

PLATE 536. Set of Baking Pans: 4½" x 11½"; 3¾" x 10"; 3½" x 8".

PLATES 537, 538, 539. Early 20th century American Tea Kettles, originally nickel plated. These kettles were made by several manufacturers in various sizes. Plate 537, 8"h, 13"d, marked "Revere Ware." Plate 538: Left, 6"h, 8"d; Right, 7"h, 10"d, porcelain finials. Plate 539, 5½"h, 6½"d, lacks lid, unusual small size.

PLATE 541. Kettle, 10"d, wooden and iron handle, wooden finial, marked "Majestic."

PLATE 540. Kettle, 7"h, tin handle, figural bird finial on spout cover, Art Deco embossed design on side.

PLATE 542. Kettle marked "Pilgrim Ware, 2 Rivers, Wis., Pat. Applied for."

PLATE 543. Kettle, wooden and copper handle, copper knob finial.

PLATE 544. Kettle, 9"h, 6½"d fancy wooden and brass handle brass finial, marked "China."

PLATE 545. Kettle, 10½" h, 10"d, lacquered, English, 19th century.

152

PLATE 546. Kettle, 9½"d, 9½"h, wooden finial, English.

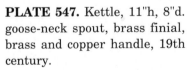

PLATE 547. Kettle, 11"h, 8"d. goose-neck spout, brass finial, brass and copper handle, 19th century.

PLATE 548. Tea Kettle, 10"d base, wide flat handle, American, circa 1920's.

PLATE 549. Tea kettle, 11"h, hammered body, goose-neck spout, circa mid 1800's.

PLATE 550. Kettle, 13"h, 6"d, goose-neck spout, brass and copper handle, brass spout, acorn finial, Victorian.

154

PLATE 551. Kettle, 11"h, 9"d, brass handle, acorn finial, lacquered.

PLATE 552. Kettle, 11½"h, 7½"d, riveted wire bail handle, European.

PLATE 553. Kettle, 8½"h, 6"d, brass handle and finial, hinged lid, European, 19th century.

PLATE 554. Kettle, 8½"h, 6"d, broad, flat handle, brass finial, English, 19th century.

PLATE 555. Kettle, 11½"h, 8"d, oval shape, goose-neck spout, 19th century.

PLATE 556. Kettle, 10½"h, 8"d, American (Frankfurt, Indiana), note wide dovetailed work around top.

PLATE 557. Kettle, 12"h, 6"d, goose-neck spout, brass and copper handle, brass acorn finial, marked "SE," 19th century.

PLATE 558. Kettle, 11½"h, 9"d, oval shaped, goose-neck spout, 19th century.

PLATE 559. Kettle, with stand and burner, initialed "C.D." on base, Victorian.

PLATE 560. Kettle with burner and pewter stand, 14½"h overall, bamboo shaped spout and legs, Victorian.

PLATE 561. Kettle, 7½"h, brass stand, burner with cover, Victorian.

PLATE 563. Tea Set: Tea Pot, Covered Hot Water Pot, Creamer, Covered Sugar Bowl, Tray; copper bodies, pewter handles, brass fittings, Victorian.

PLATE 562. Kettle, 6½"h, brass and copper; brass stand, burner missing, circa mid 20th century.

PLATE 564. Tea Urn, 18"h, brass trim; Tray, 24"l, 16"w, English, 19th century.

PLATE 565. Wine Cooler, 7"h, lacquered, originally silver plated, marked "Rep. Sheffield, Industrial Argentina," engraved Art Nouveau design on front.

PLATE 566. Egg Warmer, 10"h, pewter trim, English, Victorian.

PLATE 567. Plate Warmer, 11"d. Hot water was poured into extended opening on side.

PLATE 568. Plate Warmer with lid, 9"l, oval shaped, brass handles.

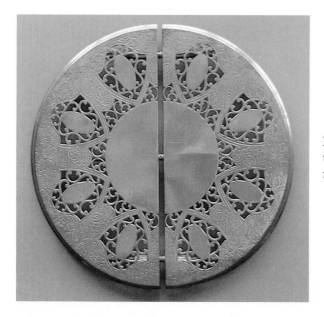

PLATE 569. Trivet, 10"d, (expands to 13"d), engraved and pierced work, marked "Royal Rochester, Sheffield."

PLATE 570. Chafing Dish, 12"h overall, pan, 9"d, copper and brass, wooden handles, ca. mid 20th century.

PLATE 571. Warming Tray, 6"h, 17"l, brass handles and legs, marked with an anchor design.

PLATE 572. Warming Tray, 33"l, 9½"w, marked "Alex Boyd & Son, Summers, 105 New Bond St., London."

PLATE 573. Centerpiece Bowl, 10"h, 11"d, lion head with ring handles, originally plated.

PLATE 574. Centerpiece, 12"d, pot metal Art Deco figure and birds, originally plated.

161

PLATE 575. Divided dish, 11¼"d, white metal border, originally plated, circa mid 20th century.

PLATE 576. Dinner Gong, 24"d, marked "Burmese." (Mounted on wooden brush holder.)

PLATE 577. Tray, 16"l, wood and copper, engraved work, English.

PLATE 578. Tray, 20½"l, 9¼"w, embossed berry and leaf pattern.

162

PLATE 579. Compote, 4½"h, 8¾"d, hammered interior with cast brass handles, marked "Art Colony Product Pure Copper," ca. 1920's.

PLATE 580. Tray, 15⅜"l overall, hammered construction from the Arts and Crafts era, marked "Schefer's Handmade Solid Copper."

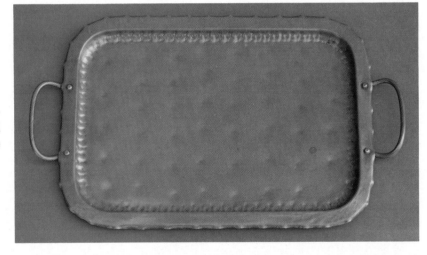

PLATE 581. Tray, 18¾"l, 11⅛"w, etched design of a ship decorates center, handmade, circa first quarter 20th century.

PLATE 582. Tray (or Salver), 12"d, spun construction, circa late 1800's to early 1900's.

PLATE 585. Tray, 15½"d, Art Nouveau desig around border, originally plated.

PLATE 583. Bowl, 2"h, 5"d, blue enameled interior, marked "China."

PLATE 586. Candle-holder, 9¼"h, brass repoussé work, originally plated.

PLATE 584. Compote, 4"h, 9"w, pierced work on outer border, originally plated.

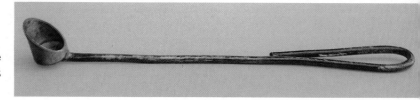

PLATE 587. Candle Snuffer, 12"l, wrought iron handle.

164

Household Copper–Bed & Bath

PLATE 588. Chamberstick, 4½"h, 5½"d, copper and brass, originally plated.

PLATE 589. Chamberstick, 4½"h, 5½"d, brass handle, 19th century.

PLATE 590. Warming Pan, 41"l, 13"d, brass top.

PLATE 591. Warming Pan, 42"l, 11"d, lacquered.

PLATE 593. Warming Pan, 46"l, 13"d, lacquered.

PLATE 592. Warming Pan, 40"l, 13"d.

PLATE 594. Bed Warmer, 12"d, brass stopper with ring handle, lacquered.

PLATE 595. Bed Warmer, 18"l, oval shaped, brass fittings, English, circa mid 19th century.

PLATE 596. Bed Warmer, 8½"d, impressed marks around top, "Wafax, Fill Completely, Reg. Design."

PLATE 597. Bed Warmer, 9"d, brass stopper, marked "Fill to Rim."

PLATE 598. Bed Warmer, 7"d, marked "Wendy, Fill to Rim."

PLATE 599. Lavabo and Cistern, brass handles and spigots, lacquered, 19th century.

167

PLATE 600. Cistern, 22"h, brass acorn finial on lid, brass spigot, English, 19th century.

PLATE 601. Cistern, 15"h, 19"l, oval shaped, brass finial and spigot.

PLATE 602. Shower Head, 8"d, pierced work around rim.

PLATE 603. Electric Heater, 11½"d, marked "The Ac. Gilbert Co., New Haven, Conn., U.S.A"

PLATE 604. Mirror, copper frame, 6½" sq. beveled glass in an easel type frame, probably used for shaving; simple cut marks around interior border form only type of decoration.

PLATE 606. Geyser, 29"h, marked "New Geysers, Ltd., London, Barralet Patents."

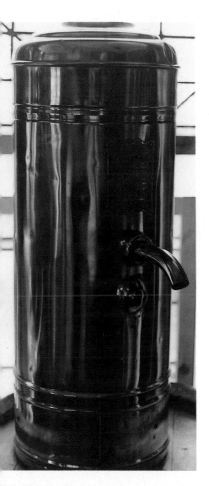

PLATE 605. Geyser, 29"h, marked "Edwarts, Victor-Geyser, London."

PLATE 607. Basin, 10½"d, spun copper, originally tinned overall, equipped with a steel hanging ring; interior remains tinned. This piece could have functioned as a basin for shaving or washing up, or even had some kitchen purpose.

PLATE 608. Child's Tub, tin base, lacquered, English.

PLATE 610. Wash Tub and Lid, 18"h, marked "Mystic Washer, Mfd. by The Kettler Mfg. Co., Houston, Texas, Patent. Pending," tin lined.

PLATE 609. Washing Machine, electric with reversible wringer, marked "Judd Laundry Machine Co., Chicago, Ill., Oct. 12, 1909.

PLATE 611. Tub, 12"h, 14"d, crude soldering visible around top.

PLATE 612. Tub, 13"h, 12"d, tin lined.

PLATE 613. Wash Tub, marked "Perco Washer, Mystic Washer Co., Houston, Texas, Patent Pending."

PLATE 614. Tub, 12"h, tin lined.

PLATE 615. Wash Boiler, marked "Atlantic 11 Gallon."

PLATE 616. Wash Boiler, 13"h, 24"l, marked "Sullivan Geiger Co., Indianapolis."

PLATE 617. Wash Boiler, 14"h, 27"l, marked "Canco."

PLATE 618. Wash Boiler, 13"h, 23"l, marked "Nesco."

PLATE 619. Wash Boiler, 13½"h, 26½"l, marked "Rochester," tin lid.

PLATE 620. Wash Boiler, 13½"h, 28½"l, copper lid.

PLATE 621. Wash Boiler, 24"l, 12"h, note original handle on right and replaced one on the left.

PLATE 622. Wash Boiler, 13"h, 25"l, unmarked.

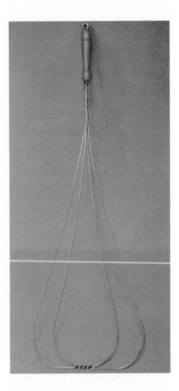

PLATE 625. Rug Beater, 30"l, wooden handle.

PLATE 623. Tub, 18"h, 27"d, lacquered.

PLATE 624. Clothes Cleaner. These were used to force hot water through the clothes.

PLATE 626. Dust Pan, 9"l, 8¼"w, embossed designs in Art Nouveau style.

Commercial Copper

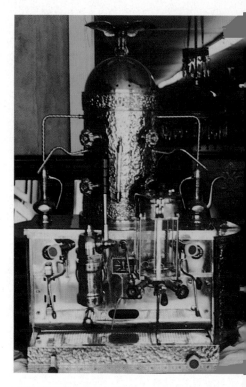

PLATE 629. Cappuccino Machine (Italian Coffee Drink), 43"h, 31"w, brass trim, marked "Brevetti Gaggia," Italian.

PLATE 627. Barber's Hot Water Container, 14"h, 11"d, contains tray for sterilizing instruments, lacquered.

PLATE 628. Double Coffee Urn, 35½"h, 25"w, three spigots, lacquered, marked "Smith St. John, Kansas City."

PLATE 630. Coffee Urn with crockery servers, 14¼"h overall, unmarked, probably German.

PLATE 631. Coffee Grinder and Dispenser, brass lid, marked "Neckzugel, Wien," Austrian.

PLATE 633. Hot Water Container, rectangular shape, iron handles, lacquered.

PLATE 632. Commercial Hot Water (or liquid) Container, 13"h, 25"l, tin top, hinged, porcelain finial, brass spigot, lacquered.

PLATE 634. Hot Water Container, 12"h, 11"d, brass spigot, iron handles, lacquered.

PLATE 635. Still, 24"h, 18½"d, brass spigot, lacquered.

PLATE 638. Brandy Warmer, 12½"h, noted as a "fireside" warmer used to heat the drink before it was served in another container.

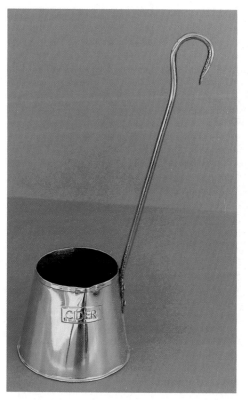

PLATE 636 & 637. Cider Measures, used by English pubs for measuring out certain amounts of the hot drink. "Cider" engraved on brass plate on front side, long iron handles, tin lined. Plate 636, 2½"h, 3"d; Plate 637, 3½"h, 3"d.

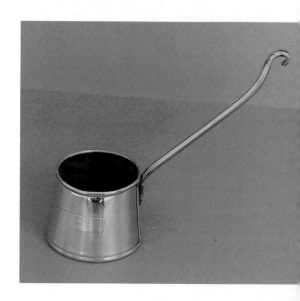

178

PLATE 639. Ale Warmer, 7½"h, 8"l, English, 19th century. The extended base was heated before serving to keep the drink warm.

PLATE 640. Tip Tray, 7¼"l, 5"w, hammered surface.

PLATE 641. Restaurant Tray, 12"d, "Jamie's" embossed in brass on border, circa mid 20th century.

PLATE 642. Cigarette Receptacle, 8"h, 12½"d, brass handles. The box holds fine grained sand.

PLATE 643. Cigarette Receptacle, 15¼"l x 10¾" x 5¾"; sheet brass with simple punched design on corners, footed, tin lined, circa 1920's.

PLATE 644. Merchant's Scale with copper shelf, marked "Doyle & Son, Borough, London, SE 1."

PLATE 645. Merchant's Scale with copper pan, iron weights, marked capacity "To Weigh 14 lbs.," 8"h overall.

PLATE 646. Printer's Plate, "Pegasus," the flying horse trademark for Magnolia Oil Co.

PLATE 647. Printer's Plate, Kiwanis emblem on left; American Legion emblem on right.

PLATE 648. Printer's Plate, "St. Louis Flower Show, 1912, Coliseum."

PLATE 649. Printer's Plate, "Hart, Schafner & Marx."

PLATE 650. Printer's Plate, advertisement for Waterspar Paint.

PLATE 651. Film Developing Tank, brass fittings.

PLATE 653. Steam Sterilizer, 21"h marked "The Arnold Steam Sterilizer—Pat. May 9, 82–April 20-97, Rochester New York." Medical instruments would have been placed inside the container and water heated in the pan below to produce the steam.

PLATE 652. Sterilizer, 18"l, insert (not shown), brass handles.

PLATE 654. Mold for
Rubber Boot, 10½"h.

PLATE 655. Mold for Rubber Boot, 14½"h.

PLATES 656, 657, 658. Molds for Leather
Cowboy Boots. 656, Left: 10½"h; 657,
Right: 13"h; 658, below: 7½"h (child's size).

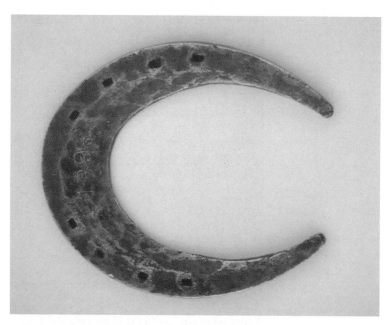

PLATE 659. Horse Shoe, 5"h, date of "1898" inscribed on the inside.

PLATE 660. Shoe Horn, 8⅞"l, handmade from hammered sheet copper, circa early 19th century.

PLATE 661. Fire Extinguisher, 24"h, (made into a lamp), marked "Quick Aid, Detroit Corp. Detroit, Michigan."

PLATE 662. Fire Extinguisher, hand pumped for pressure, 18½"h, marked "Loestrand, Rockville, Md."

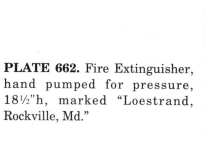

PLATE 665. Railroad Lantern, 12"h, marked "BR."

PLATE 666. Railroad Torch, 6"h. The spout held a wick.

PLATE 663. Railroad Lantern, 21"h, marked "BR (W)."

PLATE 667. Glue Pot, 6½"h, brass handles and burner attachment, electric.

PLATE 664. Lantern, 9"h, marked "S.N.L.W., Ltd.," English.

PLATE 668. Industrial Container, (unknown function), 12½"h, lacquered.

PLATE 670. Oil Can, 4"h, 3½"w, French.

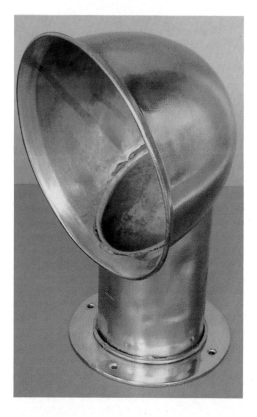

PLATE 669. Yacht Ventilator, brass base.

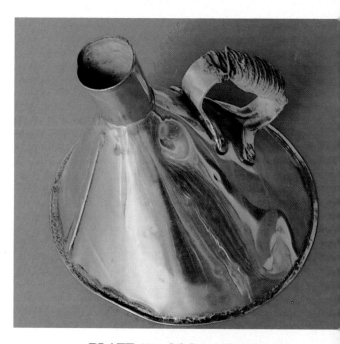

PLATE 671. Oil Can, 9"h, 9"d.

PLATE 672. Funnels. Photographs 672 through 687 show an assortment of funnels of different shapes and sizes used for various commercial, farm, or household purposes during the late 1800's to early 1900's. This one is 14"h, made with a ring for hanging.

PLATE 674. Funnel, 6"h, 6"d.

PLATE 673. Funnel, 12"h, made with a handle on side.

PLATE 675. Funnel, 6"h, triangular shaped ring for hanging.

PLATE 677. Funnel, 6½"h, 6½"d.

PLATE 676. Funnel, 9"h, 9"d, the pinch type solder seam construction is easily seen on this example.

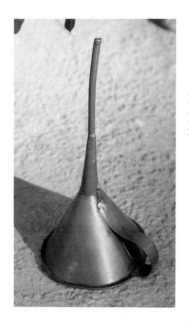

PLATE 678. Funnel, 10"h, 8"d, note how the piece has been extended by soldering the narrow part to another funnel.

PLATE 679. Funnel, 5½"h.

PLATE 681. Funnel, 8"h, rounded body with narrow cylinder shaped spout, marked "Springfield Ohio Schuler's *Static Proof* Filtering."

PLATE 680. Funnel, 14"h, 6"d, wide flat handle with rolled edge.

PLATE 682. Funnel, 3½"h, marked "Coleman No. O. Filter Funnel made in U. S. A. By Coleman Lamp & Stove." This type of funnel was used for pouring oil into the burners of a Coleman stove.

PLATE 683. Industrial Funnels, 24"h, 12½"d when joined.

PLATE 685. Funnel, 8½"h, 6"d, brass plunger.

PLATE 684. Funnel, 10½"h, 12"d.

PLATE 686. Funnel, 5½"h.

PLATE 687. Funnel, 12½"h.

PLATE 688. Flash Light, 8"l, marked "Ray-o-Vac."

PLATE 690. Soldering Iron, 13"l, copper, iron, and wood.

PLATE 689. Cow Bell, 7"h.

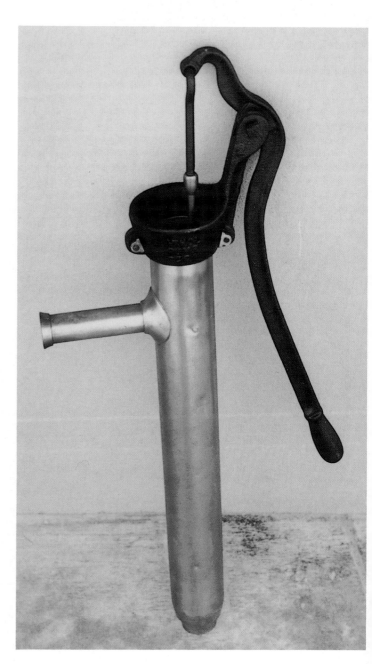

PLATE 691. Pump, 32"l, marked "Cathol, Mass."

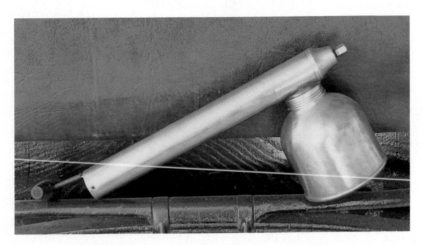

PLATE 692. Spray Pump, 14"l, copper and brass.

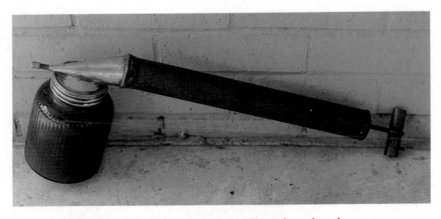

PLATE 693. Spray Pump, 19½"l, amber glass base.

Modern Reproductions

PLATE 694. Ebleskiver Pan, 8½"d, wooden handle, lacquered.

PLATE 695. Ebleskiver Pan, 7"d, iron handle.

PLATE 696. Chocolate Mold, 13"d, brass ring hook.

PLATE 697. Set of Cider Measures, brass name plates, iron handles, unlined, lacquered.

PLATE 698. Chocolate Mold, 15"l, 3¼"w, lion figures, copper plated.

PLATE 699. Ash Tray, 3½"d, brass paw feet, faked "verdigris."

PLATE 700. Cuspidor, 10"h, brass interior, marked "All Famous Havana 5¢ cigars," lacquered.

PLATE 701. Preserving Kettle, 11"h, 19"d.

PLATE 702. Umbrella Stand, 21"h, brass handles and base, lacquered.

PLATE 703. Coal Scuttle, 10"h, 16"d, "dimpled" surface.

PLATE 704. Dust Pan to match Scuttle, 13½"l, 9"w.

PLATE 705. Coal Scuttle, 16"h, hammered body, brass pedestal base, "delft-style" ceramic handle, lacquered.

PLATE 706. Weather Vane, faked "verdigris" on compass points.

PLATE 708. Lantern, marked "Anchor," brass fittings.

PLATE 707. Coal Scuttle, 17"h, ceramic "delft-style" handle, applied lion heads on each side.

PLATE 709. Ship's Light, electric, 9¼"h, marked "Hop Lee & Co., Hong Kong, No. 4751" (on brass plates on top).

Bibliography

Atterbury, Paul (ed.). *An Encyclopedia of the Decorative Arts*. London: Octopus Books, Ltd., 1979.

Baker, Stanley L. *Railroad Collectibles*, 2nd ed. Paducah, Kentucky: Collector Books, 1981.

Curtis, Anthony (comp.). *The Lyle Antiques & Their Values, Metalwork Identification & Price Guide*. Voor Hoede Publications B.V., 1982.

Dreppard, Carl. "Paul Revere, Brass and Coppersmith," in Albert Revi (ed.), *Collectible Iron, Tin, Copper & Brass*. Everybody's Press, 1974.

Franklin, Linda Campbell. *300 Years of Kitchen Collectibles*. Florence, Alabama: Books Americana, 1981.

Gaston, Mary Frank. *Antique Brass*. Paducah, Kentucky: Collector Books, 1985.

_____ . *Antique Copper*. Paducah, Kentucky: Collector Books, 1985.

Gentle, Rupert & Rachael Feild. *English Domestic Brass*. New York: E.P. Dutton and Co., Inc., 1975.

Haedeke, Hanns-Ulrich (translated by Vivienne Menkes). *Metalwork*. New York: Universe Books, 1969.

How Things Work. Vol. III. Geneva: Bibliographisches Institut and Simon and Schuster Inc., American Edition, n.d.

Jenkins, Dorothy H. "Indispensable Metals," Chapter XIV in *A Fortune in the Junk Pile*. New York: Crown Publishing, Inc., 1963.

Kauffman, Henry J. "Early American Brass and Copper and its makers," pp. 104-107 in Albert Revi (ed.), *Collectible Iron, Tin, Copper & Brass*. Everybody's Press, 1974.

_____ ."Collecting American Copper," pp. 56-58 in *Antique Trader Weekly*, December 9, 1981.

Ketchum, William C. *American Antiques*. New York: Rutledge Books, Inc., 1980.

_____ . *Western Memorabilia*. New Jersey: Hammond, 1980.

Kolter, Jane Bentley (ed.). *Early American Silver and Its Makers*. New York: Mayflower Books, Inc., 1979.

Moore, N.H. *Old Pewter, Brass, Copper & Sheffield Plate*. Garden City, New York: Garden City Publishing Company, Inc., (1905) 1933.

Mountfield, David. *The Antique Collectors' Illustrated Dictionary*. London: Hamlyn, 1974.

"Nautical Gear," pp. 98-109 in *The Encyclopedia of Collectibles*, Volume M-N. Time-Life Books, Inc., 1979.

Paley, William. "Brass Trivets—The Old and the New," pp. 111-113 in *Spinning Wheel's Collectible Iron, Tin, Copper & Brass*. Everybody's Press, Inc., 1974.

Perry, Evan. *Collecting Antique Metalware*. Garden City, New York: Doubleday & Company, Inc., 1974.

Schiffer, Peter, Nancy Schiffer and Herbert Schiffer. *The Brass Book*. Exton, Pennsylvania: Schiffer Publishing Limited, 1978.

Sears, Roebuck Catalogue (1908). Chicago, Illinois: The Gun Digest Company, 1969.

Thuro, Catherine. *Primitives & Folk Art*. Paducah, Kentucky: Collector Books, 1979.

Wills, Geoffrey. *Collecting Copper & Brass*. England: Arco Publications, 1962.

_____ . *The Book of Copper and Brass*. Feltham, England: The Hamlyn Publishing Group Limited for Country Life Books, 1968.

Index to Brass Objects

Index to Copper Objects

Value Guide

PLATE 1 ....pair $275.00 – $325.00

PLATE 2 ....$220.00 – $240.00

PLATE 3 ....pair $375.00 – $425.00

PLATE 4 ....pair $3,000.00 – $3,500.00

PLATE 5 ....$300.00 – $350.00

PLATE 6 ....pair $400.00 – $450.00

PLATE 7 ....pair $425.00 – $475.00

PLATE 8 ....pair $225.00 – $275.00

PLATE 9 ....$125.00 – $150.00

PLATE 10 ....pair $175.00 – $225.00

PLATE 11 ....pair $200.00 – $225.00

PLATE 12 ....pair $150.00 – $175.00

PLATE 13 ....pair $25.00 – $30.00

....................................centerpiece $20.00 – $25.00

PLATE 14 ....left $25.00 – $35.00

....................................right $30.00 – $35.00

....................................center $45.00 – $50.00

PLATE 15 ....pair $100.00 – $125.00

PLATE 16 ....pair $500.00 – $600.00

PLATE 17 ....$75.00 – $100.00

PLATE 18 ....pair $150.00 – $175.00

PLATE 19 ....pair $500.00 – $600.00

PLATE 20 ....each $400.00 – $500.00

PLATE 21 ....$350.00 – $450.00

PLATE 22 ....each $75.00 – $85.00

PLATE 23 ....$1,800.00 – $2,000.00

PLATE 24 ....$75.00 – $100.00

PLATE 25 ....$100.00 – $125.00

PLATE 26 ....pair $150.00 – $175.00

PLATE 27 ....pair $700.00 – $800.00

PLATE 28 ....pair $800.00 – $1000.00

PLATE 29 ....$200.00 – $250.00

PLATE 30 ....$70.00 – $80.00

PLATE 31 ....$200.00 – $250.00

PLATE 32 ....$300.00 – $350.00

PLATE 33 ....$125.00 – $150.00

PLATE 34 ....$200.00 – $225.00

PLATE 35 ....$175.00 – $200.00

PLATE 36 ....$350.00 – $450.00

PLATE 37 ....$200.00 – $250.00

PLATE 38 ....$450.00 – $550.00

PLATE 39 ....$275.00 – $300.00

PLATE 40 ....$75.00 – $100.00

PLATE 41 ....$300.00 – $350.00

PLATE 42 ....$275.00 – $300.00

PLATE 43 ....pair $200.00 – $250.00

PLATE 44 ....pair $250.00 – $300.00

PLATE 45 ....pair $400.00 – $500.00

PLATE 46 ....pair $800.00 – $1,000.00

PLATE 47 ....pair $800.00 – $1,000.00

PLATE 48 ....pair $300.00 – $400.00

PLATE 49 ....pair $450.00 – $550.00

PLATE 50 ....pair $350.00 – $450.00

PLATE 51 ....pair $200.00 – $250.00

PLATE 52 ....$325.00 – $375.00

PLATE 53 ....$800.00 – $1,000.00

PLATE 54 ....$75.00 – $85.00

PLATE 55 ....$125.00 – $150.00

PLATE 56 ....set $225.00 – $275.00

PLATE 57 ....$50.00 – $60.00

PLATE 58 ....each $40.00 – $50.00

PLATE 59 ....$200.00 – $250.00

PLATE 60 ....$200.00 – $250.00

PLATE 61 ....$500.00 – $600.00

PLATE 62 ....$225.00 – $250.00

PLATE 63 ....$125.00 – $150.00

PLATE 64 ....$175.00 – $200.00

PLATE 65 ....$200.00 – $225.00

PLATE 66 ....$120.00 – $140.00

PLATE 67 ....$125.00 – $150.00

PLATE 68 ....$400.00 – $500.00

PLATE 69 ....$800.00 – $1,000.00

PLATE 70 ....$600.00 – $800.00

PLATE 71 ....$200.00 – $225.00

PLATE 72 ....$250.00 – $300.00

PLATE 73 ....$350.00 – $400.00

PLATE 74 ....$325.00 – $375.00

PLATE 75 ....$300.00 – $350.00

PLATE 76 ....$200.00 – $250.00

PLATE 77 ....$150.00 – $175.00

PLATE 78 ....$300.00 – $350.00

PLATE 79 ....$250.00 – $275.00

PLATE 80 ....$800.00 – $1,000.00

PLATE 81 ....$100.00 – $125.00

PLATE 82 ....$175.00 – $200.00

PLATE 83 ....$100.00 – $120.00

PLATE 84 ....$150.00 – $175.00

PLATE 85 ....$200.00 – $250.00

PLATE 86 ....$200.00 – $250.00

PLATE 87 ....$150.00 – $175.00

PLATE 88 ....$75.00 – $85.00

PLATE 89 ....$75.00 – $85.00

PLATE 90 ....$65.00 – $75.00

PLATE 91 ....$75.00 – $85.00

PLATE 92 ....top $85.00 – $95.00

....................................bottom $70.00 – $80.00

PLATE 93 ....$75.00 – $85.00
PLATE 94 ....$400.00 – $450.00
PLATE 95 ....each $15.00 – $18.00
PLATE 96 ....$100.00 – $125.00
PLATE 97 ....$120.00 – $140.00
PLATE 98 ....$55.00 – $65.00
PLATE 99 ....$60.00 – $75.00
PLATE 100 ....$60.00 – $75.00
PLATE 101 ....$75.00 – $85.00
PLATE 102 ....left $85.00 – $95.00
........................right $65.00 – $75.00
PLATE 103 ....each $200.00 – $225.00
PLATE 104 ....$200.00 – $250.00
PLATE 105 ....$40.00 – $50.00
PLATE 106 ....$60.00 – $75.00
PLATE 107 ....$75.00 – $95.00
PLATE 108 ....$275.00 – $325.00
PLATE 109 ....$200.00 – $250.00
PLATE 110 ....$70.00 – $90.00
PLATE 111 ....$75.00 – $100.00
PLATE 112 ....$600.00 – $700.00
PLATE 113 ....$650.00 – $750.00
PLATE 114 ....$350.00 – $375.00
PLATE 115 ....$40.00 – $50.00
PLATE 116 ....set $300.00 – $350.00
PLATE 117 ....set $200.00 – $250.00
PLATE 118 ....$100.00 – $125.00
PLATE 119 ....$550.00 – $650.00
PLATE 120 ....$1,000.00 – $1,200.00
PLATE 121 ....$75.00 – $100.00
PLATE 122 ....$25.00 – $30.00
PLATE 123 ....$50.00 – $60.00
PLATE 124 ....pair $150.00 – $175.00
PLATE 125 ....$60.00 – $75.00
PLATE 126 ....$60.00 – $75.00
PLATE 127 ....$175.00 – $225.00
PLATE 128 ....$100.00 – $125.00
PLATE 129 ....$60.00 – $70.00
PLATE 130 ....$100.00 – $125.00
PLATE 131 ....$65.00 – $75.00
PLATE 132 ....$70.00 – $80.00
PLATE 133 ....$70.00 – $90.00
PLATE 134 ....$250.00 – $300.00
PLATE 135 ....$100.00 – $125.00
PLATE 136 ....$150.00 – $175.00
PLATE 137 ....$150.00 – $175.00
PLATE 138 ....each $35.00 – $40.00
PLATE 139 ....$100.00 – $125.00
PLATE 140 ....$75.00 – $100.00
PLATE 141 ....$100.00 – $120.00

PLATE 142 ....$125.00 – $150.00
PLATE 143 ....$110.00 – $120.00
PLATE 144 ....$100.00 – $110.00
PLATE 145 ....$45.00 – $55.00
PLATE 146 ....$40.00 – $45.00
PLATE 147 ....$125.00 – $150.00
PLATE 148 ....$125.00 – $150.00
PLATE 149 ....$250.00 – $275.00
PLATE 150 ....$110.00 – $120.00
PLATE 151 ....$30.00 – $35.00
PLATE 152 ....$25.00 – $30.00
PLATE 153 ....$35.00 – $40.00
PLATE 154 ....$30.00 – $35.00
PLATE 155 ....$150.00 – $175.00
PLATE 156 ....$400.00 – $500.00
PLATE 157 ....$200.00 – $250.00
PLATE 158 ....$40.00 – $45.00
PLATE 159 ....$120.00 – $140.00
PLATE 160 ....$85.00 – $95.00
PLATE 161 ....$250.00 – $350.00
PLATE 162 ....$175.00 – $225.00
PLATE 163 ....$85.00 – $95.00
PLATE 164 ....$125.00 – $175.00
PLATE 165 ....$130.00 – $140.00
PLATE 166 ....$120.00 – $140.00
PLATE 167 ....$1,300.00 – $1,500.00
PLATE 168 ....$1,400.00 – $1,600.00
PLATE 169 ....$260.00 – $280.00
PLATE 170 ....$300.00 – $325.00
PLATE 171 ....$1,200.00 – $1,300.00
PLATE 172 ....$100.00 – $120.00
PLATE 173 ....$2,200.00 – $2,400.00
PLATE 174 ....$1,200.00 – $1,400.00
PLATE 175 ....$65.00 – $75.00
PLATE 176 ....$30.00 – $35.00
PLATE 177 ....$55.00 – $60.00
PLATE 178 ....$140.00 – $160.00
PLATE 179 ....$150.00 – $175.00
PLATE 180 ....$10.00 – $12.00
PLATE 181 ....$80.00 – $90.00
PLATE 182 ....$90.00 – $100.00
PLATE 183 ....right $120.00 – $140.00
...................top $100.00 – $120.00
...................foreground $70.00 – $90.00
PLATE 184 ....$30.00 – $40.00
PLATE 185 ....$60.00 – $70.00
PLATE 186 ....$75.00 – $85.00
PLATE 187 ....$60.00 – $75.00
PLATE 188 ....$80.00 – $100.00
PLATE 189 ....$250.00 – $275.00

PLATE 190 ....$150.00 – $175.00
PLATE 191 ....each $150.00 – $175.00
PLATE 192 ....$45.00 – $55.00
PLATE 193 ....$120.00 – $140.00
PLATE 194 ....$35.00 – $40.00
PLATE 195 ....left $20.00 – $25.00
..........................center $40.00 – $45.00
............................right $80.00 – $85.00
PLATE 196 ....each $45.00 – $55.00
PLATE 197 ....$45.00 – $55.00
PLATE 198 ....$35.00 – $40.00
PLATE 199 ....$40.00 – $45.00
PLATE 200 ....$20.00 – $25.00
PLATE 201 ....$150.00 – $175.00
PLATE 202 ....$350.00 – $400.00
PLATE 203 ....$25.00 – $30.00
PLATE 204 ....$25.00 – $35.00
PLATE 205 ....$275.00 – $300.00
PLATE 206 ....$225.00 – $250.00
PLATE 207 ....Lamp $100.00 – $125.00
................Shell itself $30.00 – $35.00
PLATE 208 ....$1,000.00 – $1,200.00
PLATE 209 ....$800.00 – $1,000.00
PLATE 210 ....$55.00 – $65.00
PLATE 211 ....$40.00 – $50.00
PLATE 212 ....$450.00 – $550.00
PLATE 213 ....$75.00 – $85.00
PLATE 214 ....$400.00 – $500.00
PLATE 215 ....$300.00 – $350.00
PLATE 216 ....$400.00 – $500.00
PLATE 217 ....$450.00 – $550.00
PLATE 218 ....$900.00 – $1,000.00
PLATE 219 ....$800.00 – $1,000.00
PLATE 220 ....$800.00 – $1,000.00
PLATE 221 ....$1,500.00 – $1,600.00
PLATE 222 ....$175.00 – $200.00
PLATE 223 ....$200.00 – $225.00
PLATE 224 ....$160.00 – $175.00
PLATE 225 ....$35.00 – $40.00
PLATE 226 ....$70.00 – $75.00
PLATE 227 ....$20.00 – $25.00
PLATE 228 ....$450.00 – $500.00
PLATE 229 ....$120.00 – $140.00
PLATE 230 ....$275.00 – $300.00
PLATE 231 ....$400.00 – $450.00
PLATE 232 ....$300.00 – $350.00
PLATE 233 ....$125.00 – $150.00
PLATE 234 ....$55.00 – $65.00
PLATE 235 ....$50.00 – $60.00
PLATE 236 ....$75.00 – $100.00

PLATE 237 ....$150.00 – $175.00
PLATE 238 ....$45.00 – $55.00
PLATE 239 ....$70.00 – $90.00
PLATE 240 ....each $25.00 – $35.00
PLATE 241 ....each $60.00 – $75.00
PLATE 242 ....left $55.00 – $65.00
............................right $40.00 – $50.00
PLATE 243 ....each $25.00 – $35.00
PLATE 244 ....left $12.00 – $15.00
..........................center $60.00 – $75.00
............................right $25.00 – $30.00
PLATE 245 ....each $10.00 – $15.00
PLATE 246 ....each $20.00 – $30.00
PLATE 247 ....each $15.00 – $18.00
PLATE 248 ....each $20.00 – $25.00
PLATE 249 ....each $15.00 – $18.00
PLATE 250 ....top $20.00 – $25.00
........................bottom $35.00 – $40.00
PLATE 251 ....left $45.00 – $55.00
............................right $30.00 – $40.00
PLATE 252 ....top pair $45.00 – $55.00
................center pair $55.00 – $65.00
..............bottom pair $65.00 – $75.00
PLATE 253................left $20.00 – $25.00
..........................center $25.00 – $30.00
..............................left $20.00 – $25.00
PLATE 254 ....each $30.00 – $35.00
PLATE 255 ....left $30.00 – $35.00
..................right pair $25.00 – $30.00
PLATE 256 ....$150.00 – $175.00
PLATE 257 ....$70.00 – $80.00
PLATE 258 ....$65.00 – $75.00
PLATE 259 ....$120.00 – $140.00
PLATE 260 ....$45.00 – $55.00
PLATE 261 ....$75.00 – $85.00
PLATE 262 ....$15.00 – $18.00
PLATE 263 ....$450.00 – $500.00
PLATE 264 ....$1,200.00 – $1,500.00
PLATE 265 ....$3,000.00 – $3,500.00
PLATE 266 ....$700.00 – $800.00
PLATE 267 ....$250.00 – $300.00
PLATE 268 ....$250.00 – $300.00
PLATE 269 ....$300.00 – $350.00
PLATE 270 ....$375.00 – $400.00
PLATE 271 ....$175.00 – $200.00
PLATE 272 ....$40.00 – $50.00
PLATE 273 ....$50.00 – $65.00
PLATE 274 ....$300.00 – $350.00
PLATE 275 ....$60.00 – $70.00
PLATE 276 ....$25.00 – $30.00

PLATE 277 ....$40.00 – $50.00	PLATE 327 ....each $75.00 – $85.00
PLATE 278 ....$70.00 – $80.00	PLATE 328 ....$15.00 – $20.00
PLATE 279 ....$150.00 – $175.00	PLATE 329 ....$50.00 – $65.00
PLATE 280 ....$500.00 – $600.00	PLATE 330 ....each $5.00 – $8.00
PLATE 281 ....pair $275.00 – $325.00	PLATE 331 ....$100.00 – $125.00
PLATE 282 ....pair $125.00 – $150.00	PLATE 332 ....$30.00 – $40.00
PLATE 283 ....pair $50.00 – $65.00	PLATE 333 ....$120.00 – $140.00
PLATE 284 ....$300.00 – $350.00	PLATE 334 ....$55.00 – $65.00
PLATE 285 ....$350.00 – $400.00	PLATE 335 ....$60.00 – $70.00
PLATE 286 ....set $150.00 – $200.00	PLATE 336 ....$25.00 – $35.00
PLATE 287 ....$60.00 – $75.00	PLATE 337 ....$70.00 – $80.00
PLATE 288 ....$175.00 – $200.00	PLATE 338 ....$70.00 – $80.00
PLATE 289 ....$200.00 – $225.00	PLATE 339 ....$25.00 – $30.00
PLATE 290 ....$600.00 – $700.00	PLATE 340 ....pair $100.00 – $125.00
PLATE 291 ....$75.00 – $90.00	PLATE 341 ....$45.00 – $55.00
PLATE 292 ....$300.00 – $350.00	PLATE 342 ....$15.00 – $20.00
PLATE 293 ....$80.00 – $90.00	PLATE 343 ....$25.00 – $30.00
PLATE 294 ....$200.00 – $225.00	PLATE 344 ....$50.00 – $60.00
PLATE 295 ....$45.00 – $55.00	PLATE 345 ....$25.00 – $30.00
PLATE 296 ....$35.00 – $45.00	PLATE 346 ....$60.00 – $65.00
PLATE 297 ....$75.00 – $100.00	PLATE 347 ....$25.00 – $30.00
PLATE 298 ....each $25.00 – $35.00	PLATE 348 ....$150.00 – $175.00
PLATE 299 ....each $25.00 – $35.00	PLATE 349 ....$300.00 – $400.00
PLATE 300 ....each $10.00 – $12.00	PLATE 350 ....$1,200.00 – $1,400.00
PLATE 301 ....$225.00 – $275.00	PLATE 351 ....$300.00 – $350.00
PLATE 302 ....$60.00 – $75.00	PLATE 352 ....$175.00 – $200.00
PLATE 303 ....$175.00 – $200.00	PLATE 353 ....each $15.00 – $18.00
PLATE 304 ....$800.00 – $1,000.00	PLATE 354 ....$125.00 – $150.00
PLATE 305 ....$800.00 – $1,000.00	PLATE 355 ....$55.00 – $65.00
PLATE 306 ....$500.00 – $600.00	PLATE 356 ....$275.00 – $300.00
PLATE 307 ....$1,200.00 – $1,400.00	PLATE 357 ....$350.00 – $375.00
PLATE 308 ....$35.00 – $45.00	PLATE 358 ....$125.00 – $150.00
PLATE 309 ....$40.00 – $45.00	PLATE 359 ....$125.00 – $150.00
PLATE 310 ....$55.00 – $65.00	PLATE 360 ....$150.00 – $175.00
PLATE 311 ....$40.00 – $50.00	PLATE 361 ....$50.00 – $60.00
PLATE 312 ....$175.00 – $200.00	PLATE 362 ....$40.00 – $50.00
PLATE 313 ....$150.00 – $175.00	PLATE 363 ....$125.00 – $150.00
PLATE 314 ....$450.00 – $500.00	PLATE 364 ....$120.00 – $140.00
PLATE 315 ....$70.00 – $80.00	PLATE 365 ....$250.00 – $300.00
PLATE 316 ....$60.00 – $75.00	PLATE 366 ....$500.00 – $600.00
PLATE 317 ....$25.00 – $35.00	PLATE 367 ....$2,500.00 – $2,800.00
PLATE 318 ....pair $350.00 – $400.00	PLATE 368 ....$100.00 – $125.00
PLATE 319 ....each $60.00 – $75.00	PLATE 369 ....$250.00 – $300.00
PLATE 320 ....$65.00 – $75.00	PLATE 370 ....$1,200.00 – $1,400.00
PLATE 321 ....pair $150.00 – $175.00	PLATE 371 ....set $275.00 – $325.00
PLATE 322 ....pair $100.00 – $125.00	PLATE 372 ....$225.00 – $250.00
PLATE 323 ....$150.00 – $175.00	PLATE 373 ....set $450.00 – $500.00
PLATE 324 ....$250.00 – $300.00	PLATE 374 ....$250.00 – $275.00
PLATE 325 ....$400.00 – $500.00	PLATE 375 ....$225.00 – $250.00
PLATE 326 ....$85.00 – $100.00	PLATE 376 ....$175.00 – $200.00

PLATE 377 ....$175.00 – $200.00

PLATE 378 ....$1,400.00 – $1,600.00

PLATE 379 ....$250.00 – $275.00

PLATE 380 ....$2,200.00 – $2,500.00

PLATE 381 ....$400.00 – $500.00

PLATE 382 ....$140.00 – $160.00

PLATE 383 ....$50.00 – $60.00

PLATE 384 ....$200.00 – $250.00

PLATE 385 ....$175.00 – $200.00

PLATE 386 ....$125.00 – $150.00

PLATE 387 ....$75.00 – $85.00

PLATE 388 ....$25.00 – $30.00

PLATE 389 ....$40.00 – $50.00

PLATE 390 ....$300.00 – $400.00

PLATE 391 ....$120.00 – $140.00

PLATE 392 ....$35.00 – $45.00

PLATE 393 ....pair $30.00 – $40.00

PLATE 394 ....pair $350.00 – $450.00

PLATE 395 ....pair $275.00 – $325.00

PLATE 396 ....$70.00 – $90.00

PLATE 397 ....$175.00 – $225.00

PLATE 398 ....$400.00 – $500.00

PLATE 399 ....set $100.00 – $125.00

PLATE 400 ....$50.00 – $60.00

PLATE 401 ....each $20.00 – $25.00

PLATE 402 ....$125.00 – $150.00

PLATE 403 ....each $200.00 – $225.00

PLATE 404 ....each $15.00 – $20.00

PLATE 405 ....$140.00 – $160.00

PLATE 406 ....$25.00 – $30.00

PLATE 407 ....$65.00 – $75.00

PLATE 408 ....$40.00 – $50.00

PLATE 409 ....$300.00 – $350.00

PLATE 410 ....set $175.00 – $200.00

PLATE 411 ....$175.00 – $200.00

PLATE 412 ....$10.00 – $12.00

PLATE 413 ....$20.00 – $25.00

PLATE 414 ....$350.00 – $400.00

PLATE 415 ....$225.00 – $250.00

PLATE 416 ....$100.00 – $125.00

PLATE 417 ....$100.00 – $125.00

PLATE 418 ....$100.00 – $125.00

PLATE 419 ....$350.00 – $400.00

PLATE 420 ....$20.00 – $25.00

PLATE 421 ....$50.00 – $60.00

PLATE 422 ....$55.00 – $65.00

PLATE 423 .... Percolator $300.00 – $350.00

............Sugar and Creamer set $125.00 – $150.00

PLATE 424 ....$300.00 – $325.00

PLATE 425 ....$350.00 – $400.00

PLATE 426 ....$150.00 – $175.00

PLATE 427 ....$135.00 – $150.00

PLATE 428 ....$140.00 – $150.00

PLATE 429 ....$75.00 – $100.00

PLATE 430 ....$250.00 – $300.00

PLATE 431 ....$300.00 – $350.00

PLATE 432 ....$450.00 – $500.00

PLATE 433 ....$120.00 – $140.00

PLATE 434 ....$100.00 – $125.00

PLATE 435 ....$225.00 – $250.00

PLATE 436 ....$35.00 – $45.00

PLATE 437 ....$100.00 – $125.00

PLATE 438 ....left $70.00 – $80.00

.............................right $50.00 – $60.00

PLATE 439 ....$125.00 – $135.00

PLATE 440 ....$70.00 – $80.00

PLATE 441 ....$90.00 – $100.00

PLATE 442 ....$90.00 – $100.00

PLATE 443 ....$80.00 – $90.00

PLATE 444 ....$125.00 – $150.00

PLATE 445 ....$300.00 – $350.00

PLATE 446 ....Kettle and Stand $450.00 – $500.00

.........................Stirrer $50.00 – $65.00

PLATE 447 ....$300.00 – $350.00

PLATE 448 ....$125.00 – $150.00

PLATE 449 ....$125.00 – $150.00

PLATE 450 ....$150.00 – $175.00

PLATE 451 ....$325.00 – $350.00

PLATE 452 ....$275.00 – $300.00

PLATE 453 ....$275.00 – $300.00

PLATE 454 ....$125.00 – $150.00

PLATE 455 ....$70.00 – $90.00

PLATE 456 ....$150.00 – $175.00

PLATE 457 ....$150.00 – $175.00

PLATE 458 ....$150.00 – $175.00

PLATE 459 ....$200.00 – $225.00

PLATE 460 ....$200.00 – $225.00

PLATE 461 ....$300.00 – $350.00

PLATE 462 ....$225.00 – $250.00

PLATE 463 ....$200.00 – $225.00

PLATE 464 ....$120.00 – $140.00

PLATE 465 ....$80.00 – $100.00

PLATE 466 ....left $140.00 – $150.00

.....................center $120.00 – $130.00

.........................right $90.00 – $100.00

PLATE 467 ....left (back row) $135.00 – $150.00

....center (back row) $120.00 – $130.00

......right (back row) $110.00 – $120.00

...........left (front row) $80.00 – $90.00

.......center (front row) $70.00 – $80.00

..........right (front row) $60.00 – $70.00
PLATE 468 ....$140.00 – $160.00
PLATE 469 ....$120.00 – $135.00
PLATE 470 ....left $20.00 – $25.00
..........................right $15.00 – $20.00
PLATE 471 ....$425.00 – $450.00
PLATE 472 ....$350.00 – $375.00
PLATE 473 ....$250.00 – $275.00
PLATE 474 ....$200.00 – $225.00
PLATE 475 ....$250.00 – $275.00
PLATE 476 ....$325.00 – $350.00
PLATE 477 ....$400.00 – $425.00
PLATE 478 ....$175.00 – $200.00
PLATE 479 ....$200.00 – $225.00
PLATE 480 ....$45.00 – $55.00
PLATE 481 ....$140.00 – $160.00
PLATE 482 ....$225.00 – $250.00
PLATE 483 ....$225.00 – $250.00
PLATE 484 ....$200.00 – $225.00
PLATE 485 ....$100.00 – $125.00
PLATE 486 ....$250.00 – $275.00
PLATE 487 ....$275.00 – $300.00
PLATE 488 ....$120.00 – $140.00
PLATE 489 ....$45.00 – $55.00
PLATE 490 ....$120.00 – $140.00
PLATE 491 ....$100.00 – $125.00
PLATE 492 ....$100.00 – $125.00
PLATE 493 ....$140.00 – $160.00
PLATE 494 ....$175.00 – $200.00
PLATE 495 ....$100.00 – $125.00
PLATE 496 ....$65.00 – $75.00
PLATE 497 ....$200.00 – $225.00
PLATE 498 ....$125.00 – $150.00
PLATE 499 ....$75.00 – $100.00
PLATE 500 ....$55.00 – $65.00
PLATE 501 ....$200.00 – $225.00
PLATE 502 ....$125.00 – $150.00
PLATE 503 ....left $80.00 – $90.00
.....................center $70.00 – $80.00
..........................right $50.00 – $60.00
PLATE 504 ....$70.00 – $90.00
PLATE 505 ....$275.00 – $325.00
PLATE 506 ....$400.00 – $500.00
PLATE 507 ....$250.00 – $300.00
PLATE 508 ....$300.00 – $350.00
PLATE 509 ....$550.00 – $650.00
PLATE 510 ....$175.00 – $225.00
PLATE 511 ....$225.00 – $275.00
PLATE 512 ....$800.00 – $900.00
PLATE 513 ....$175.00 – $200.00

PLATE 514 ....$375.00 – $425.00
PLATE 515 ....$250.00 – $300.00
PLATE 516 ....$150.00 – $175.00
PLATE 517 ....$225.00 – $250.00
PLATE 518 ....$400.00 – $450.00
PLATE 519 ....$200.00 – $225.00
PLATE 520 ....$225.00 – $250.00
PLATE 521 ....set $350.00 – $400.00
PLATE 522 ....$150.00 – $175.00
PLATE 523 ....$300.00 – $325.00
PLATE 524 ....$225.00 – $250.00
PLATE 525 ....$225.00 – $250.00
PLATE 526 ....$225.00 – $250.00
PLATE 527 ....$250.00 – $275.00
PLATE 528 ....$150.00 – $175.00
PLATE 529 ....$450.00 – $500.00
PLATE 530 ....$150.00 – $175.00
PLATE 531 ....$80.00 – $90.00
PLATE 532 ....$250.00 – $275.00
PLATE 533 ....$125.00 – $150.00
PLATE 534 ....$160.00 – $180.00
PLATE 535 ....left $55.00 – $65.00
..........................right $70.00 – $80.00
PLATE 536 ....bottom $125.00 – $150.00
.....................center $110.00 – $125.00
..........................top $80.00 – $100.00
PLATE 537 ....$80.00 – $90.00
PLATE 538 ....left $60.00 – $70.00
..........................right $65.00 – $75.00
PLATE 539 ....$50.00 – $60.00
PLATE 540 ....$75.00 – $85.00
PLATE 541 ....$70.00 – $80.00
PLATE 542 ....$170.00 – $190.00
PLATE 543 ....$75.00 – $85.00
PLATE 544 ....$175.00 – $200.00
PLATE 545 ....$200.00 – $225.00
PLATE 546 ....$140.00 – $160.00
PLATE 547 ....$250.00 – $275.00
PLATE 548 ....$65.00 – $75.00
PLATE 549 ....$175.00 – $200.00
PLATE 550 ....$200.00 – $250.00
PLATE 551 ....$225.00 – $275.00
PLATE 552 ....$75.00 – $95.00
PLATE 553 ....$175.00 – $225.00
PLATE 554 ....$150.00 – $200.00
PLATE 555 ....$250.00 – $300.00
PLATE 556 ....$275.00 – $325.00
PLATE 557 ....$250.00 – $300.00
PLATE 558 ....$275.00 – $325.00
PLATE 559 ....$300.00 – $400.00

PLATE 560 ....$350.00 – $450.00
PLATE 561 ....$300.00 – $400.00
PLATE 562 ....$225.00 – $275.00
PLATE 563 ....set $275.00 – $325.00
PLATE 564 ....set $3,000.00 – $3,200.00
PLATE 565 ....$120.00 – $140.00
PLATE 566 ....$200.00 – $250.00
PLATE 567 ....$225.00 – $275.00
PLATE 568 ....$300.00 – $350.00
PLATE 569 ....$70.00 – $80.00
PLATE 570 ....$150.00 – $175.00
PLATE 571 ....$375.00 – $425.00
PLATE 572 ....$300.00 – $350.00
PLATE 573 ....$80.00 – $90.00
PLATE 574 ....$300.00 – $350.00
PLATE 575 ....$65.00 – $75.00
PLATE 576 ....$275.00 – $325.00
PLATE 577 ....$70.00 – $85.00
PLATE 578 ....$120.00 – $140.00
PLATE 579 ....$60.00 – $75.00
PLATE 580 ....$75.00 – $100.00
PLATE 581 ....$75.00 – $100.00
PLATE 582 ....$60.00 – $75.00
PLATE 583 ....$30.00 – $40.00
PLATE 584 ....$40.00 – $50.00
PLATE 585 ....$70.00 – $90.00
PLATE 586 ....$80.00 – $90.00
PLATE 587 ....$35.00 – $40.00
PLATE 588 ....$70.00 – $80.00
PLATE 589 ....$70.00 – $80.00
PLATE 590 ....$300.00 – $350.00
PLATE 591 ....$325.00 – $375.00
PLATE 592 ....$300.00 – $350.00
PLATE 593 ....$325.00 – $375.00
PLATE 594 ....$200.00 – $225.00
PLATE 595 ....$700.00 – $800.00
PLATE 596 ....$50.00 – $60.00
PLATE 597 ....$80.00 – $90.00
PLATE 598 ....$50.00 – $60.00
PLATE 599 ....$3,200.00 – $3,500.00
PLATE 600 ....$800.00 – $900.00
PLATE 601 ....$275.00 – $325.00
PLATE 602 ....$70.00 – $80.00
PLATE 603 ....$75.00 – $90.00
PLATE 604 ....$40.00 – $55.00
PLATE 605 ....$250.00 – $350.00
PLATE 606 ....$250.00 – $350.00
PLATE 607 ....$100.00 – $125.00
PLATE 608 ....$450.00 – $550.00
PLATE 609 ....$1,800.00 – $2,000.00

PLATE 610 ....$150.00 – $175.00
PLATE 611 ....$65.00 – $75.00
PLATE 612 ....$70.00 – $80.00
PLATE 613 ....$100.00 – $125.00
PLATE 614 ....$100.00 – $125.00
PLATE 615 ....$140.00 – $160.00
PLATE 616 ....$100.00 – $125.00
PLATE 617 ....$70.00 – $90.00
PLATE 618 ....$120.00 – $140.00
PLATE 619 ....$100.00 – $125.00
PLATE 620 ....$150.00 – $175.00
PLATE 621 ....$80.00 – $100.00
PLATE 622 ....$120.00 – $140.00
PLATE 623 ....$225.00 – $250.00
PLATE 624 ....$30.00 – $35.00
PLATE 625 ....$40.00 – $55.00
PLATE 626 ....$40.00 – $50.00
PLATE 627 ....$350.00 – $400.00
PLATE 628 ....$1,200.00 – $1,400.00
PLATE 629 ....$1,000.00 – $1,200.00
PLATE 630 ....$300.00 – $400.00
PLATE 631 ....$700.00 – $800.00
PLATE 632 ....$225.00 – $275.00
PLATE 633 ....$250.00 – $300.00
PLATE 634 ....$175.00 – $225.00
PLATE 635 ....$450.00 – $500.00
PLATE 636 ....$115.00 – $125.00
PLATE 637 ....$115.00 – $125.00
PLATE 638 ....$150.00 – $175.00
PLATE 639 ....$200.00 – $250.00
PLATE 640 ....$15.00 – $18.00
PLATE 641 ....$30.00 – $40.00
PLATE 642 ....$225.00 – $250.00
PLATE 643 ....$150.00 – $175.00
PLATE 644 ....$200.00 – $250.00
PLATE 645 ....$225.00 – $275.00
PLATE 646 ....$45.00 – $55.00
PLATE 647 ....left $15.00 – $18.00
........................right $25.00 – $30.00
PLATE 648 ....$35.00 – $45.00
PLATE 649 ....$35.00 – $40.00
PLATE 650 ....$25.00 – $30.00
PLATE 651 ....$40.00 – $50.00
PLATE 652 ....$275.00 – $325.00
PLATE 653 ....$200.00 – $225.00
PLATE 654 ....$175.00 – $200.00
PLATE 655 ....$125.00 – $150.00
PLATE 656 ....$150.00 – $175.00
PLATE 657 ....$125.00 – $150.00
PLATE 658 ....$100.00 – $125.00

PLATE 659 ....$30.00 – $35.00	PLATE 679 ....$15.00 – $20.00
PLATE 660 ....$45.00 – $55.00	PLATE 680 ....$30.00 – $35.00
PLATE 661 ....$200.00 – $225.00	PLATE 681 ....$35.00 – $40.00
PLATE 662 ....$100.00 – $125.00	PLATE 682 ....$25.00 – $30.00
PLATE 663 ....$175.00 – $200.00	PLATE 683 ....$45.00 – $55.00
PLATE 664 ....$125.00 – $150.00	PLATE 684 ....$20.00 – $25.00
PLATE 665 ....$100.00 – $125.00	PLATE 685 ....$30.00 – $35.00
PLATE 666 ....$60.00 – $75.00	PLATE 686 ....$20.00 – $25.00
PLATE 667 ....$125.00 – $150.00	PLATE 687 ....$125.00 – $135.00
PLATE 668 ....$30.00 – $40.00	PLATE 688 ....$35.00 – $40.00
PLATE 669 ....$75.00 – $100.00	PLATE 689 ....$15.00 – $20.00
PLATE 670 ....$50.00 – $60.00	PLATE 690 ....$15.00 – $20.00
PLATE 671 ....$70.00 – $80.00	PLATE 691 ....$225.00 – $250.00
PLATE 672 ....$35.00 – $40.00	PLATE 692 ....$45.00 – $55.00
PLATE 673 ....$45.00 – $50.00	PLATE 693 ....$85.00 – $100.00
PLATE 674 ....$30.00 – $35.00	
PLATE 675 ....$15.00 – $20.00	
PLATE 676 ....$35.00 – $40.00	
PLATE 677 ....$20.00 – $25.00	Note: Prices are not quoted for Reproductions, Plates
PLATE 678 ....$25.00 – $30.00	694 – 709.

Other Books by Mary Frank Gaston

The Collector's Encyclopedia of Limoges Porcelain, Second Edition $24.95

The Collector's Encyclopedia of R. S. Prussia $24.95

The Collector's Encyclopedia of R. S. Prussia, Second Series $24.95

The Collector's Encyclopedia of Flow Blue China $19.95

Blue Willow, Revised Edition $14.95

American Belleek $19.95

Art Deco $14.95

These titles may be ordered from the author or publisher.
Please add $2.00 for the 1st and 30¢ for each additional book.

Mary Frank Gaston
P.O. Box 342   or
Bryan, TX 77806-0342

Collector Books
P.O. Box 3009
Paducah, KY 42002-3009

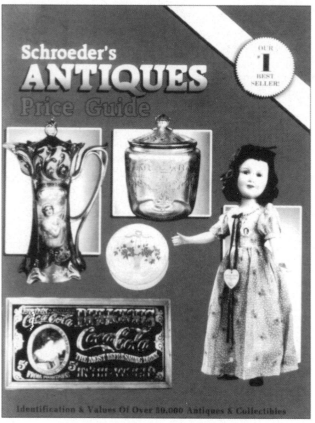